10 STEP DRAWING

Dogs

Published in 2022 by Search Press Ltd.
Wellwood, North Farm Road
Tunbridge Wells
Kent TN2 3DR

Reprinted 2023, 2024, 2025

This book is produced by
The Bright Press, an imprint of the Quarto Group,
1 Triptych Place, London
SE1 9SH, United Kingdom.
T (0)20 7700 6700
www.quarto.com

Our EU representation is covered by information on our website
GPSR information can be found at www.searchpress.com

ISBN: 978-1-80092-034-7
ebook ISBN: 978-1-80093-027-8

Conceived, designed and produced by The Bright Press,
an imprint of Quarto Publishing plc

Publisher: James Evans
Editorial Director: Isheeta Mustafi
Art Director: James Lawrence
Managing Editor: Jacqui Sayers
Development Editor: Abbie Sharman
Project Editor: Polly Goodman
Design: JC Lanaway

10 9 8 7 6 5 4

Printed in Guandong, China

Dogs

DRAW OVER (50) DELIGHTFUL DOGS
IN 10 EASY STEPS

JUSTINE LECOUFFE

Search Press

Contents

≫≫ Faces & features

≫≫ Dogs at rest

>>> Dogs in motion

>>> Dogs & puppies

Introduction

In this book, you will find more than 50 illustrations of beautiful dogs and adorable puppies that have been created in just ten simple steps. So, whether it's a tall Irish Wolfhound, a tiny Chihuahua or a cheeky Jack Russell wanting to play ball, it's time to choose your favourite canine companion and get drawing!

TACKLING DIFFERENT SHAPES

Dogs and puppies come in all different shapes and sizes. The step-by-step instructions in this book show you how to use simple shapes and outlines as guides for placing heads, limbs and wagging tails. This will enable you to get the proportions right.

At the beginning of each chapter, you will find a guide for drawing basic head shapes, facial features and poses. Once you've mastered the basics, you can move on to applying these techniques to more than 50 different breeds. Follow the instructions and guides for the shapes of the heads, bodies, legs and tails to help you achieve a realistic appearance for different breeds, as well as a variety of natural poses, from lying on their backs to catching a ball.

I have also provided a colour palette at the end of each finished drawing. Use this as a guide, but feel free to experiment with coat colours to adapt your pooch pictures as desired.

I hope you will enjoy creating the images in this book as much as I did. Drawing dogs has never been easier!

How to use this book

BASIC EQUIPMENT

Paper: Any paper will do, but sketch paper will give you the best results.

Pencil, eraser and pencil sharpener: Try different pencil grades and invest in a good-quality eraser and sharpener.

Coloured pencils: A good set of coloured pencils, with about twenty-four shades, is really all you need.

Small ruler: This is optional, but you may find it useful for drawing guidelines.

FOLLOWING THE STEPS

Use pencil to trace the shape guidelines in each step. Use a dark-coloured pencil to add the outlines and details. Then erase the underlying pencil. Finally, apply colour as you like.

COLOURING

You have several options when it comes to colouring your drawings – why not explore them all?

Pencils: This is the simplest option, and the one I have chosen for finishing the pictures in this book.

Stay inside the lines and keep your pencils sharp so you have control in the smaller areas.

To achieve a lighter or darker shade, try layering the colour or pressing harder with your pencil.

Dog fur comes in different colours and has different patterns and textures, so once you're confident with where the shading should be on each one, try varying the tones you use.

Paint and brush: Watercolour is probably easiest to work with for beginners, although using acrylic or oil means that you can paint over any mistakes. You'll need two or three brushes of different sizes, with at least one very fine brush.

Faces & features

Front view:
Head

Mastering these simple steps will give you the basic skills to build
up a portrait drawing of your favourite four-legged friend.

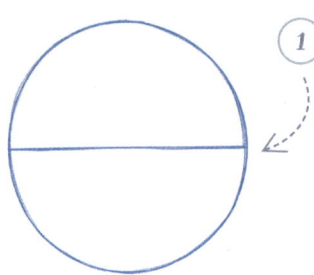

1 Draw a circle guide. Add
a straight horizontal line
across the centre.

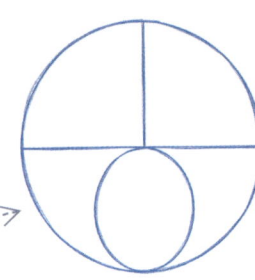

2 Draw a vertical line through
the centre of the upper half.
Add an oval shape to help
place the muzzle.

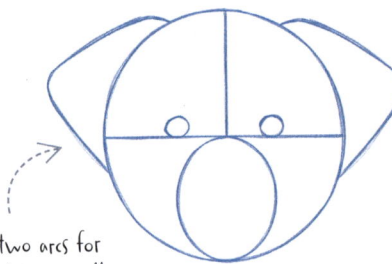

3 Draw two arcs for
ears and two small
circles for eyes.

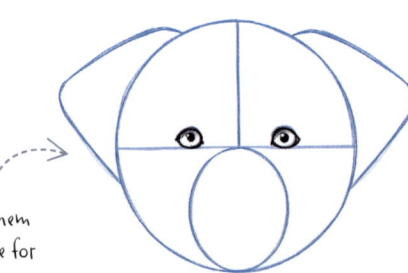

4 Darken the eyes, giving them
pointed edges. Add a circle for
each pupil, with another
tiny reflection circle inside.

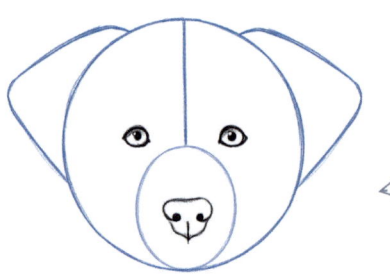

5 Draw the top edge of the nose using a
wavy line. Make the sides curve inwards
as you darken the lines to create nostrils.
Make the bottom tip pointy and add a
short, vertical line, splitting the bottom of
the nose in half.

6 For the mouth, draw two lines that split and curve towards each edge of the oval guide. Follow the bottom edge to draw the chin.

7 Darken the ears, using short strokes for a fur effect.

8 Use the main circle as a guide to draw the rest of the head. Trace the inner path of the circle as you draw the sides, under the ears.

9 Erase your guidelines. Add strokes for extra detail around the face and to create the markings.

10 Add a light brown base colour, with darker tones towards the chin and tips of the ears. Use darker brown tones for the nose and eyes. Keep the muzzle and forehead markings white, or use a light tone.

Side view:
Head

Adapt the length of the muzzle to suit the breed of dog you are drawing.
Here, on this Collie, the muzzle is quite long.

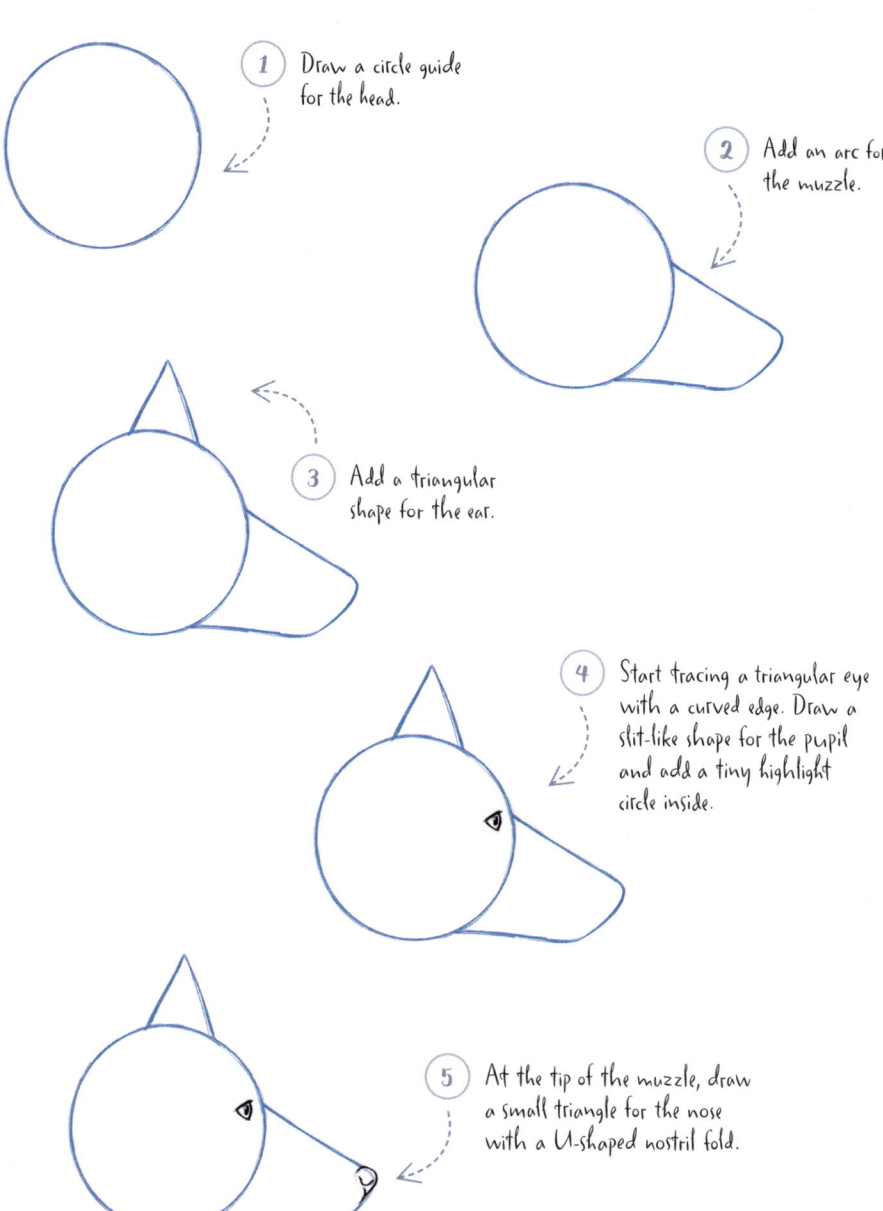

1. Draw a circle guide for the head.

2. Add an arc for the muzzle.

3. Add a triangular shape for the ear.

4. Start tracing a triangular eye with a curved edge. Draw a slit-like shape for the pupil and add a tiny highlight circle inside.

5. At the tip of the muzzle, draw a small triangle for the nose with a U-shaped nostril fold.

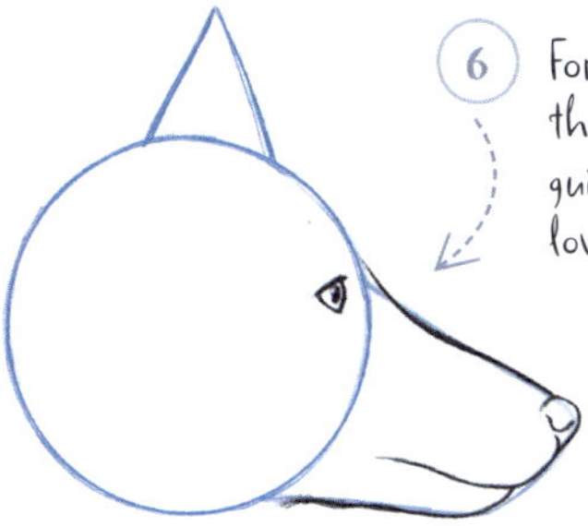

6 For the mouth, draw a line that curves to the left, almost to the edge of the circle guide. Add short strokes to create a furry lower jaw.

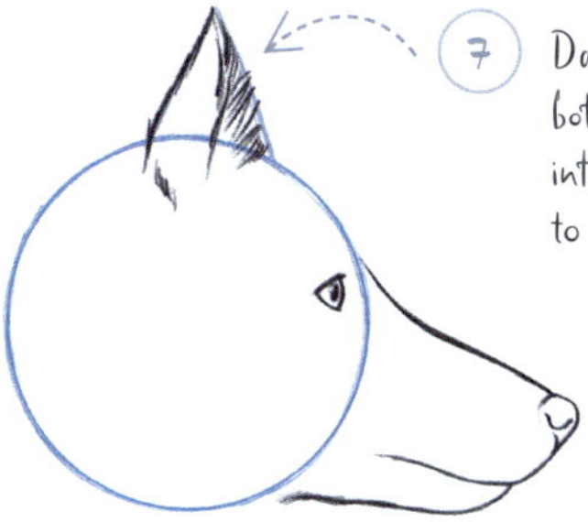

7 Darken the ear, making the bottom longer so it stretches into the head. Add short strokes to create the furry ear opening.

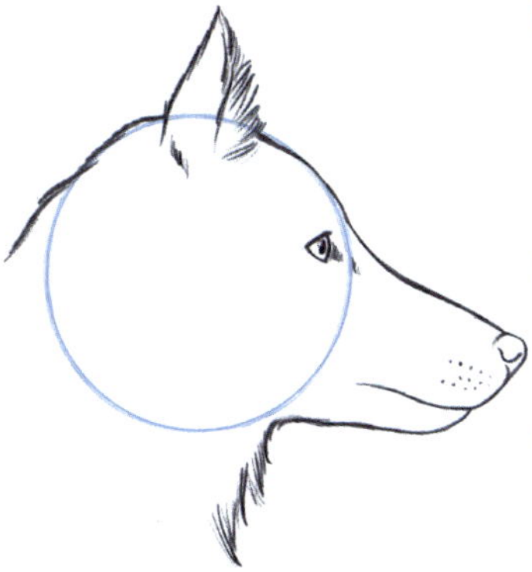

8 Draw the neck and the rest of the head, and add a few dots above the mouth and short lines beside the eye.

9 Erase your guidelines. Add short strokes around the face, and longer strokes for the hair on the back of the head and neck.

10 Use light brown as a base colour, and darker brown tones for the eyes and nose. Finish with darker tones towards the nose, ear and back of the head.

Eyes

For best results, ensure the eyes are at the same height on the face and roughly the same distance from the centre.

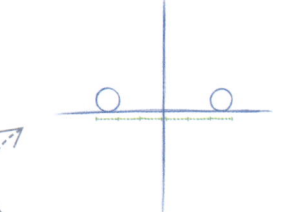

1 Draw two crossing guidelines to help with alignment and symmetry. As the dotted lines show, there is about twice the length of the diameter between the vertical line and each circle.

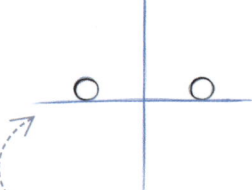

2 Draw two circles on the horizontal guidelines.

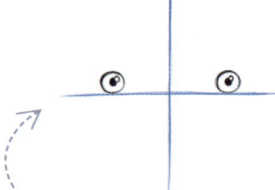

3 Add two small circles for pupils, and a tiny circle on one side for the light reflection.

14

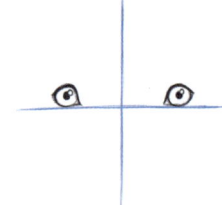

4 Shape the eyelids around the circles, making the edges pointy.

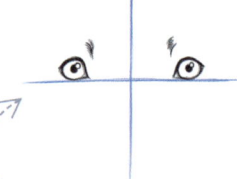

5 Add short lines at the top for the eyebrows. These help with expression.

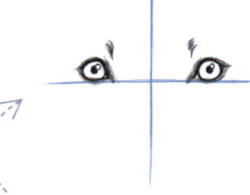

6 Refine the outlines of the eyes, making the bottom lines and top eyelids thicker and darker. Erase your guidelines.

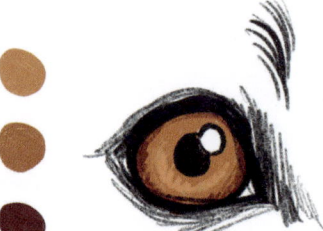
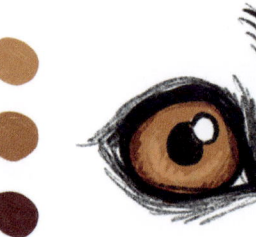

7 When adding colour, use darker tones on the outer edges and lighter tones towards the centre.

Nose

These simple steps will give your canine companion
a perfectly formed nose and mouth every time.

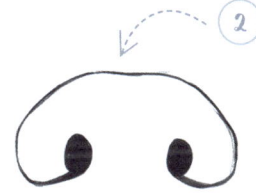

1. Trace two small circles for
the nostrils. Shade them in,
adding an outward curve
on each side.

2. Darken the top edge
using a wavy line.

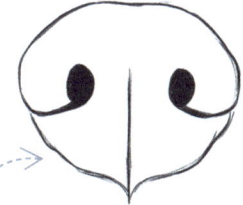

3. Add a vertical line towards the middle
and curved lines on each side, going
up to the sides of the nose.

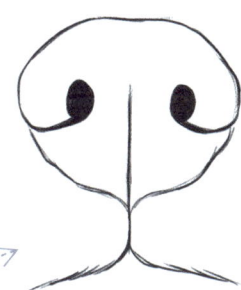

4. Split the vertical line into two
lines for the mouth, using
short strokes to resemble fur.

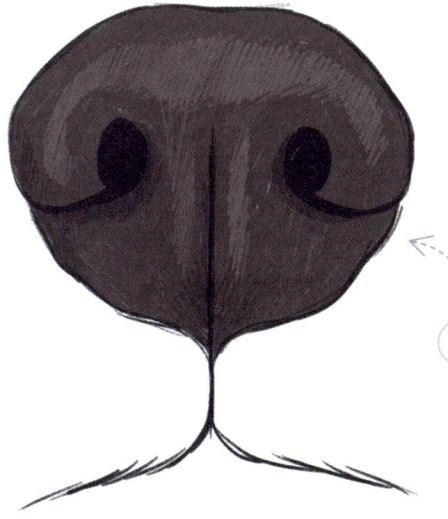

5. Colour the nose dark brown, with lighter
tones to show where the light falls.

Ears

When sketching the ears, do not follow your arc guidelines too strictly
or they will not look natural. Short pencil strokes give the ears
some movement.

Pricked ears

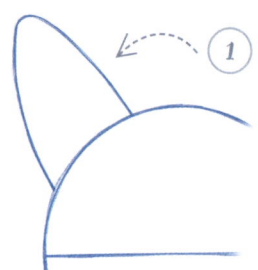

1. Trace an arc on top of the head.

2. Roughly draw around the guidelines using short strokes.

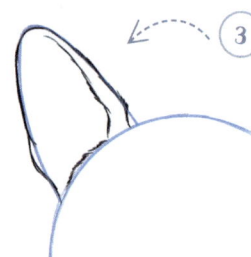

3. Add another line, parallel to the ear outline. This is where the ear folds and it delineates the inside of the ear.

4. Erase your guidelines. Add small strokes inside the ear to create depth.

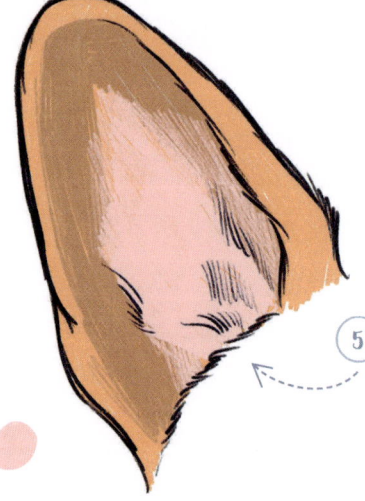

5. Colour the centre pink. Use a darker brown around the inside of the ear and a lighter brown on the outside.

Folded ears

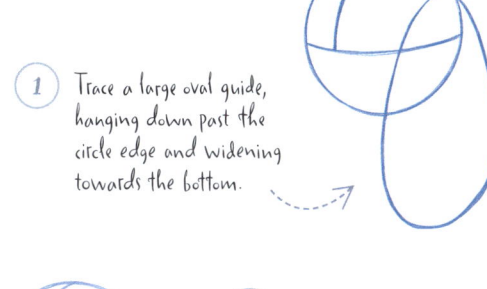

1 Trace a large oval guide, hanging down past the circle edge and widening towards the bottom.

2 Draw roughly around the guidelines using short strokes.

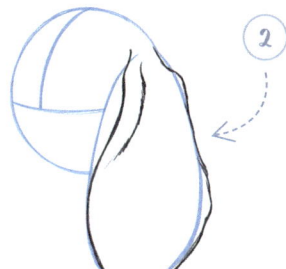

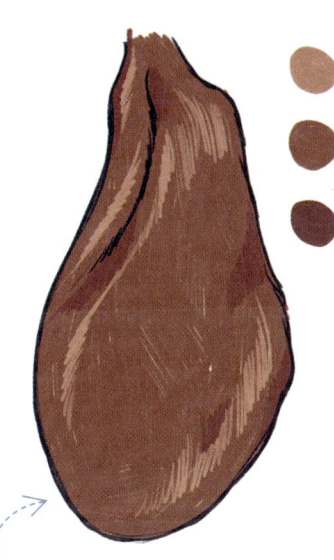

3 Colour the ear, adding highlights at the top and towards the edges.

Drop ears

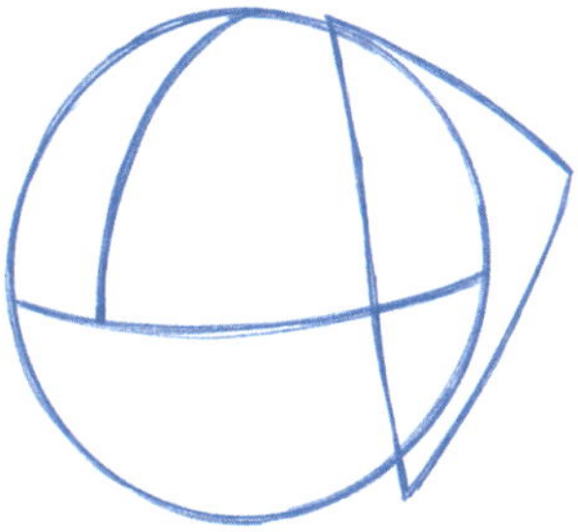

1 Trace a triangular guide from the top to the bottom of your circle guide.

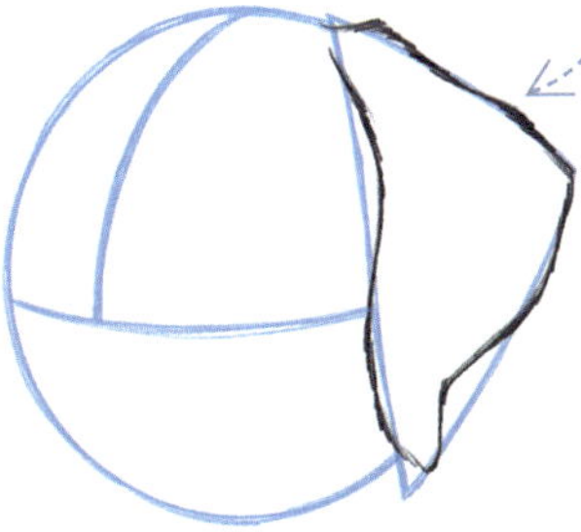

2 Draw roughly around the guidelines using short strokes, making the bottom of the ear narrower and more pointed.

3 Erase your guidelines. Add small strokes to indicate the curves and depth.

4 Colour the ear, adding darker details and lighter tones to resemble fur.

Labrador Retriever

Labs are good-natured, sweet-faced and high-spirited. To achieve their silky-smooth fur, shade smoothly instead of using separate strokes.

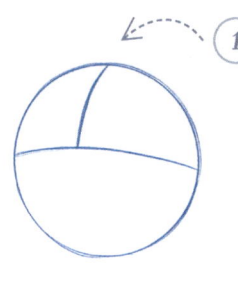

(1) Draw a circle guide, adding a curved, horizontal line across the centre and a curved, vertical line through the top half.

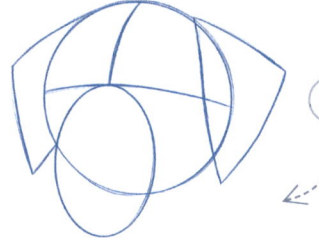

(2) Add an oval for the muzzle guide. Add triangles for the ears (part of the left ear is hidden behind the head).

(3) Draw two short lines for the neck. Sketch two small circles for the eyes, adding the pupils and tiny circles for highlights. The left eye should be smaller than the right.

(4) Sketch the nose. Add a vertical line at the bottom to split the lower section in half. The right nostril should be slightly larger than the left.

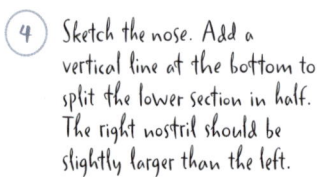

(5) Follow the lower edge of the circle to draw a wavy line for the right side of the top lip and a smaller curve for the left side.

6 Draw the chin, tongue and two lower teeth with curved lines, keeping the muzzle mostly within the initial oval. Draw the right ear using short strokes for a fur-like texture.

7 Draw the rest of the head. Use short strokes to darken the lines under the head and create the neck.

8 Draw the left ear. Add small strokes on the ears and neck to create fur.

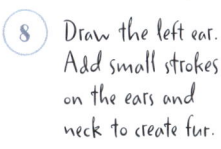

9 Erase your guidelines. Add a beige or light yellow base tone.

10 Use a darker tone to create shadows on the ears, neck and around the eyes. Add dark grey for the mouth and nose, light brown for the eyes and pink for the tongue.

Siberian Husky

The husky's piercing blue eyes, thick coat and striking features
only add to the appeal of this graceful Siberian breed.

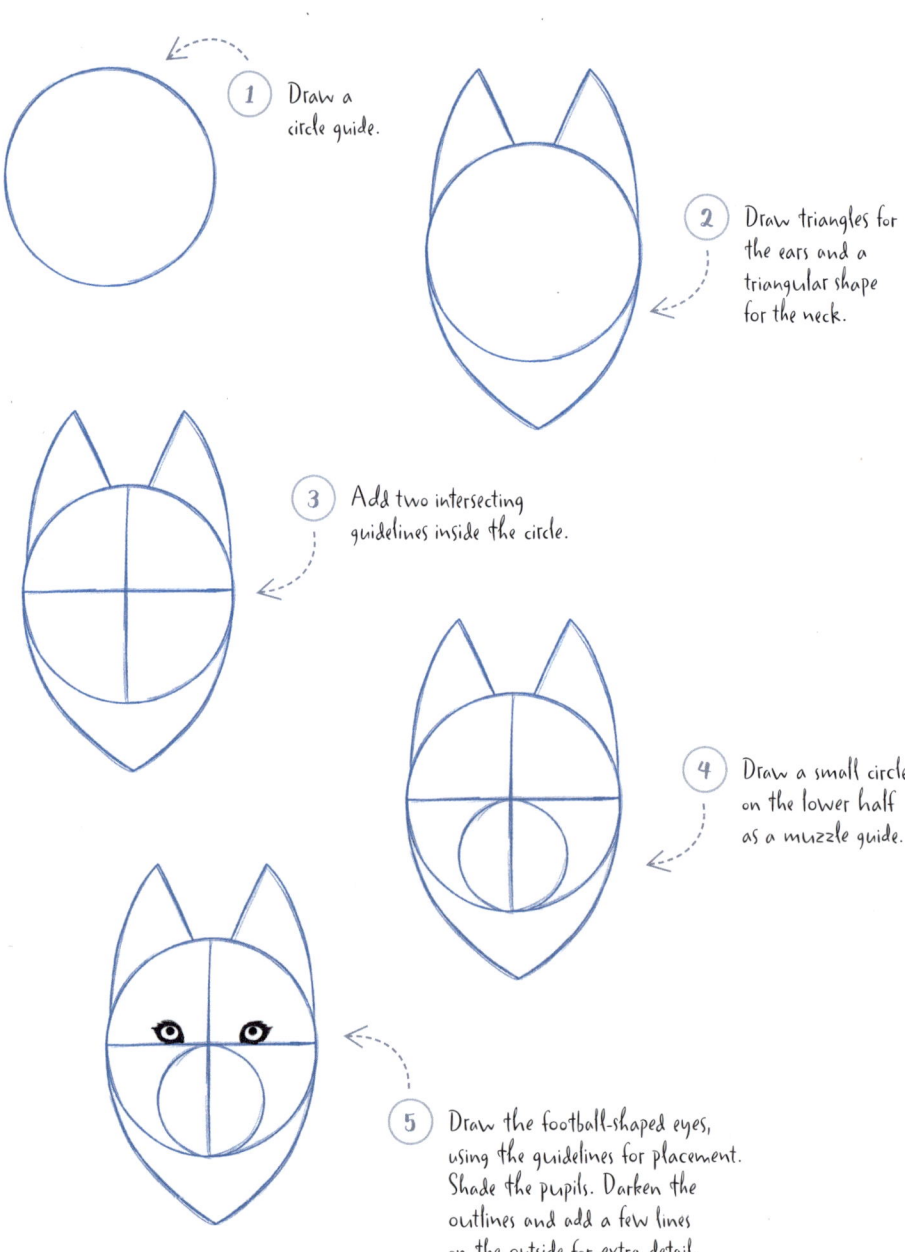

1. Draw a circle guide.

2. Draw triangles for the ears and a triangular shape for the neck.

3. Add two intersecting guidelines inside the circle.

4. Draw a small circle on the lower half as a muzzle guide.

5. Draw the football-shaped eyes, using the guidelines for placement. Shade the pupils. Darken the outlines and add a few lines on the outside for extra detail.

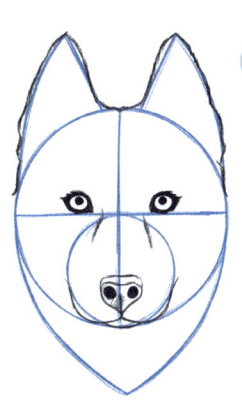

6 Draw two nostrils and a few lines surrounding the nose. Draw a line below the nose that splits it in two and curls up to form the mouth, and another line for the chin. Draw the ears, using quick, short strokes.

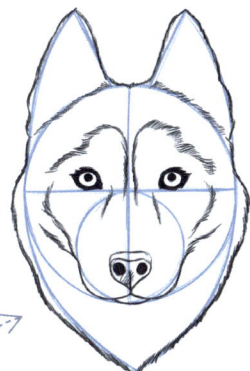

8 Erase your guidelines. Add small strokes for the ear openings. Add shading under the chin and around the eyes, ears and neck, to help create dimension.

7 Shape the rest of the head, using quick, short strokes. Add short strokes around the eyes and muzzle.

9 Add colour. Huskies have a light fur with dark grey accents on top of their ears and head.

10 Add light brown to create shadows on the neck and ears. Finish with light blue eyes.

Cavalier King Charles Spaniel

While Cavaliers come in four colours, the beautiful Blenheim, as depicted here, is the most common: a rich chestnut on a pearly white background.

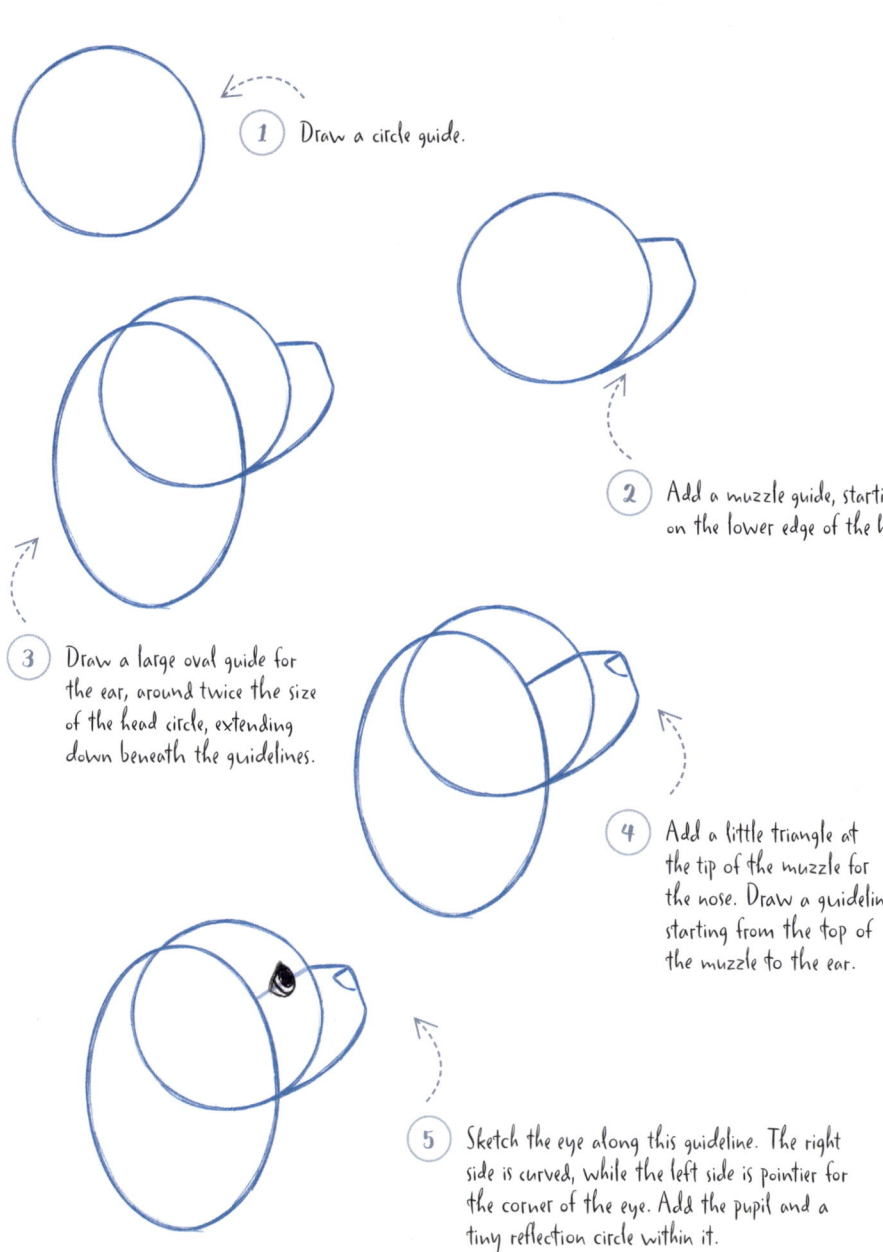

1 Draw a circle guide.

2 Add a muzzle guide, starting on the lower edge of the head.

3 Draw a large oval guide for the ear, around twice the size of the head circle, extending down beneath the guidelines.

4 Add a little triangle at the tip of the muzzle for the nose. Draw a guideline starting from the top of the muzzle to the ear.

5 Sketch the eye along this guideline. The right side is curved, while the left side is pointier for the corner of the eye. Add the pupil and a tiny reflection circle within it.

6 Draw the nose, following the muzzle guideline.

7 Follow the circle guide to draw the rest of the head, using short strokes on the forehead.

8 Draw the ear, making the edges curvier as you darken the guidelines. Along the bottom edge, add short, vertical lines for the tips of the fur.

9 Erase your guidelines. Add the neck fur, using short strokes under the chin to the same length as the ear. Colour the head and neck in light beige, the ear and area around the eye in light brown, the eye in dark brown and the nose in dark grey.

10 For more dimension and volume, add some shading using darker and lighter values.

Boston Terrier

Boston Terriers have a sleek, shiny coat with crisp white markings
in a pattern that resembles a tuxedo – part of the reason they
gained the nickname 'American Gentleman'.

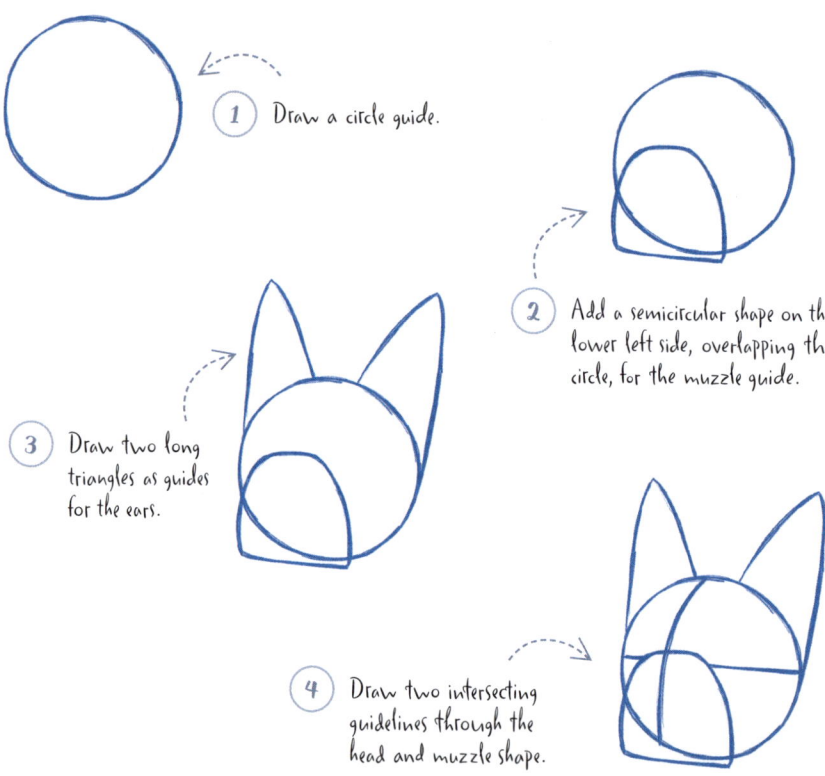

(1) Draw a circle guide.

(2) Add a semicircular shape on the lower left side, overlapping the circle, for the muzzle guide.

(3) Draw two long triangles as guides for the ears.

(4) Draw two intersecting guidelines through the head and muzzle shape.

(5) Draw the eyes, using the guidelines for placement. Add large dots for the pupils and tiny reflection circles to the sides. Add eyebrows, then draw the nose.

24

6 Follow the guidelines to draw the rest of the muzzle. Draw a line below the nose that splits in two and curls up to form the mouth.

7 Use the two arcs as guides to draw the ears. Use minimal strokes to represent short hair. Draw around the head, following the circle guide.

8 Erase your guidelines. Draw the neck and markings.

9 Use dark grey for the ears, nose and around the eyes. Colour the eyes brown. Leave the rest of the head white, or colour it in a very light grey tone.

10 Colour the inside of the ears pink. To create dimension, add shading under the chin and around the eyes, ears and neck.

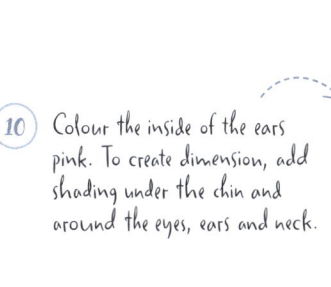

English Springer Spaniel

Developed as gun dogs, English Springer Spaniels are tough, muscular hunters, but they also make popular companions – highly affectionate and full of energy.

(1) Draw a circle guide, with a horizontal line across the centre.

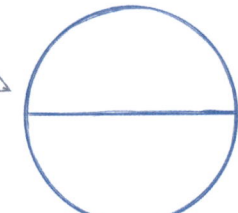

(2) For the muzzle guide, start with a line going left from the base of the circle (a). Go diagonally up to the left for about half the length (b) and finish with a diagonal line reaching the top of the circle (c).

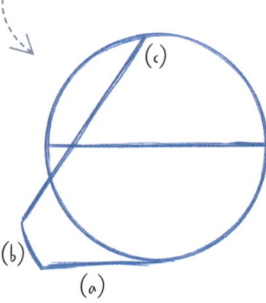

(3) Draw a curve from the lower side of the muzzle guide to the centre of the bottom edge as a guide for the lower jaw.

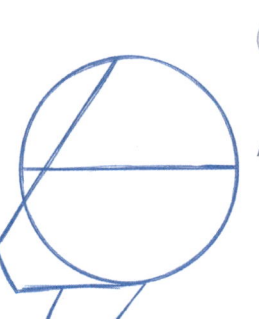

(4) On each side of the head circle, add curved shapes for the ears.

(5) Position the eyes along the horizontal guideline and the nose at the tip of the muzzle.

6 Draw the lower lip, chin and tongue using a series of curved lines. Add a few pointy teeth.

7 Use short strokes to darken the guidelines from the muzzle to the top of the head.

8 Follow the basic path of the ears, using short strokes for a fur-like texture. Add small strokes within the ears to create fur.

9 Erase your guidelines. Add some strokes in the middle of the head to create the markings.

10 Colour the face and ears a reddish brown, leaving the markings, muzzle, teeth and neck white. The nose is flecked with ticking – small, isolated areas of brown hairs. Add dark brown to the nose, pink to the tongue and light brown to the eyes.

Border Collie

Border Collies are energetic, intelligent working dogs, bred for herding sheep.
They are known for their intense stare, with which they control their flock.

(1) Draw a circle guide, with a central horizontal line.

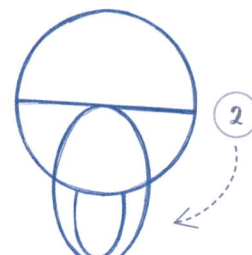

(2) Add a vertical oval shape for the muzzle and a U-shape below the circle guide for the tongue.

(3) Draw a large, curved V-shape for the neckline.

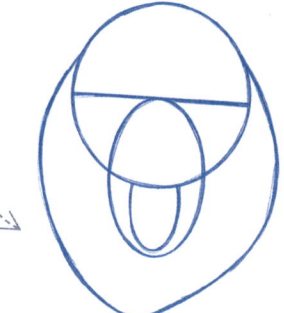

(4) Draw two large triangles as guides for the ears.

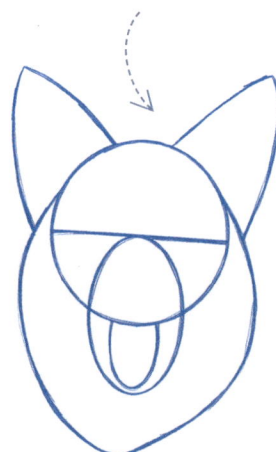

(5) Draw football-shaped eyes, using the guidelines for placement. Shade a small circle in each eye for the pupils. Draw the nose, with two small C-shapes on either side for nostrils.

6 Following the muzzle guide, draw a line below the nose that splits in two and curls up to form the mouth. Add lines for the tongue and lower jaw.

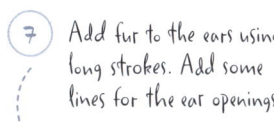

7 Add fur to the ears using long strokes. Add some lines for the ear openings.

8 Shape the rest of the head using long strokes for a furry look.

9 Erase your guidelines. Prepare the markings by adding some short strokes between the eyes and around the muzzle and neck.

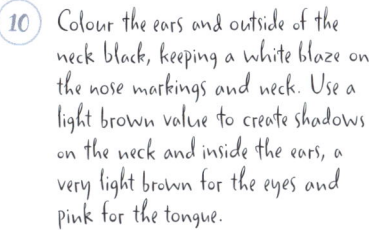

10 Colour the ears and outside of the neck black, keeping a white blaze on the nose markings and neck. Use a light brown value to create shadows on the neck and inside the ears, a very light brown for the eyes and pink for the tongue.

Labradoodle

The Labradoodle is a smart, sociable cross between a Poodle and a Labrador Retriever. This lovable chap has found a stick and is eager to play!

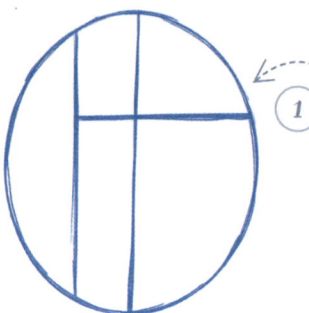

1 Draw a vertical oval as a guide. Draw two straight vertical lines down, and a shorter horizontal line across the top third.

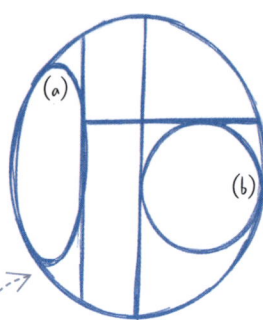

2 Draw a long oval on the left side as a guide for the ear (a). Draw a circle for the muzzle on the right, beneath the horizontal line (b).

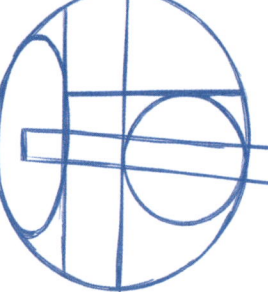

3 Sketch a long rectangle for the stick.

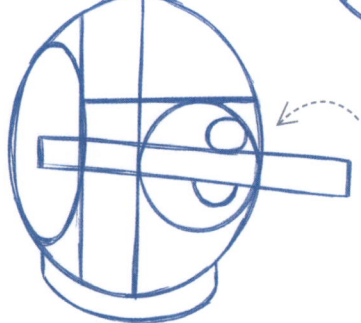

4 On the top and bottom of the rectangle, within the muzzle circle, add an oval and a semi-circle to help you position the nose and mouth.

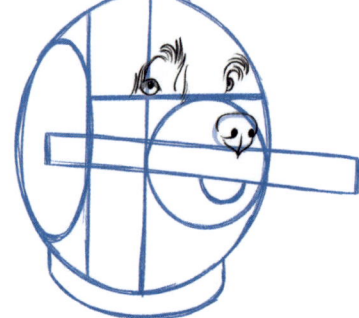

5 Sketch the eyes on top of the horizontal guideline, with the left eye positioned on the central vertical guideline. The right eye should be smaller than the left, as the head is slightly turned. Add the eyebrow hair, which partly covers the eyes, and draw the nose.

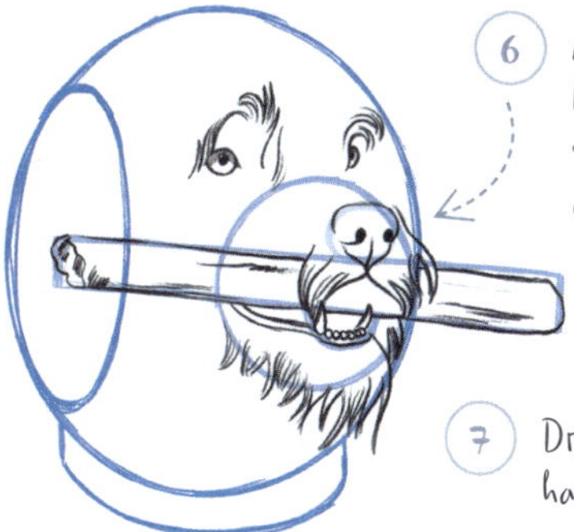

6 Add curved strokes under the nose for the hairy front of the muzzle. Draw the stick, then add the mouth and lower jaw, with a series of longer hairs below.

7 Draw the ears, with long hairs around the bottom. Add curved strokes for the back of the muzzle, and a line from the nostril to indicate the top.

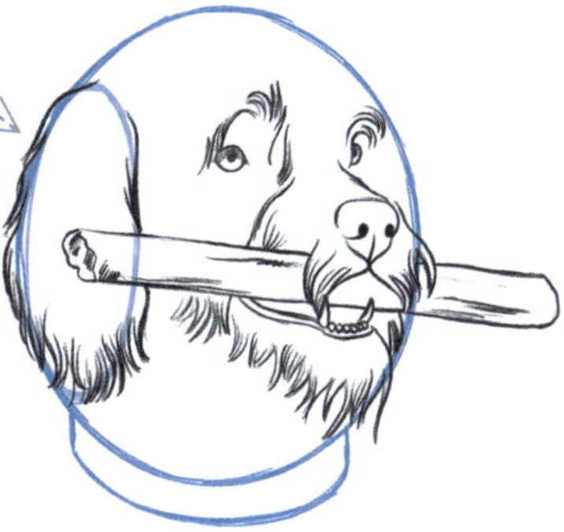

8 Draw the rest of the head, using short strokes to darken the lines under the head. Add the neck and collar.

9 Erase your guidelines. Colour the top of the head light beige, using a slightly darker value to create shadows.

10 Vary the pressure on your pencil for different degrees of tonal value. Add dark brown to the mouth, nose and eyes; light beige for the stick; and a bright colour for the collar.

Italian Greyhound

The Italian Greyhound was the favourite companion of noblewomen in the Middle Ages, particularly in Italy. With its graceful looks and doting temperaments, it is easy to see why.

1. Draw a circle guide, adding a long, curved, horizontal line across the centre and a shorter, curved, vertical line through the left of the top half.

3. Draw triangular shapes on each side for ear guidelines.

2. Add a rectangular shape for the muzzle.

4. For the neck, draw two vertical lines below the head, and a third curved line to join them.

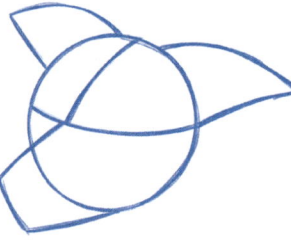

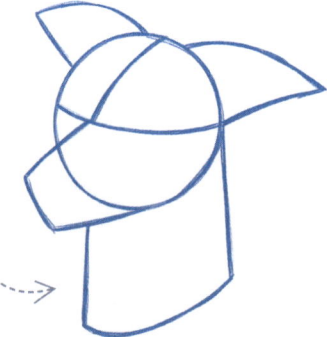

5. Sketch the eyes, sitting on top of the horizontal guideline, at either side of the vertical line. The left eye should be smaller than the right, as the head is slightly turned.

6 Lightly sketch the nose, adding a vertical line to split the lower section in half.

7 Follow the basic path of the ear guides using curved lines.

8 Draw the top lip as a wavy line from the bottom of the nose. Add dots above the top lip. Follow the guide for the chin below. Draw the rest of the head and neck using short strokes.

9 Erase your guidelines. Add small lines around the eyes, under the chin and on the ears.

10 Colour the muzzle area light beige. Use light grey for the head and neck, adding darker shading inside the ears and along the neck. Colour the nose dark grey and the eyes brown.

Staffordshire Bull Terrier

Staffordshire Bull Terriers are known for their intelligence, courage and love of children. Who could resist this friendly face?

1. Draw a rectangular guide.

2. Draw a semicircle under it, and two triangles as guides for ears.

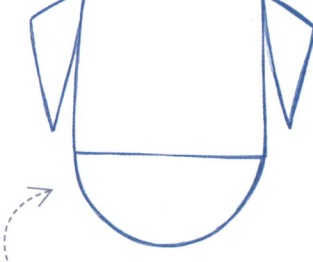

3. Draw a vertical line in the middle of the head, and add a second horizontal line above the first. Draw a curved line below for the neck.

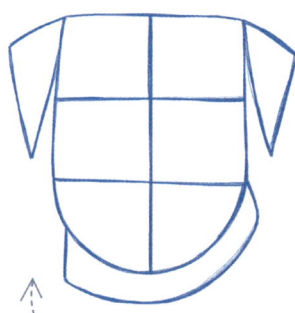

4. Sketch the eyes sitting on top of the horizontal guideline at either side of the vertical line. Add the nose in the centre along the vertical line.

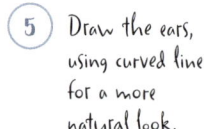

5. Draw the ears, using curved lines for a more natural look.

6 Add a few small lines above the nose. Draw two lines below the horizontal line that split from the bottom of the nose and curve back up.

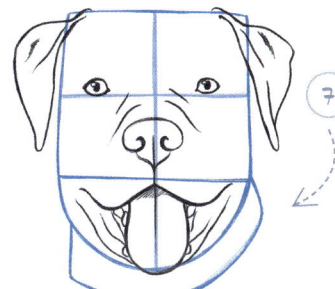

7 Draw the chin within the bottom semicircle, using a series of curved lines. Add the tongue.

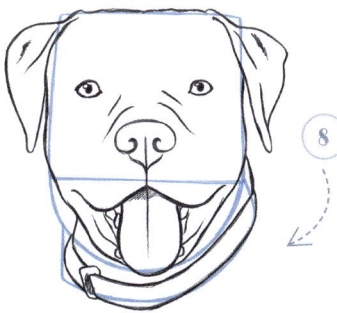

8 Use the rectangular guide to draw the rest of the head. Use short strokes to darken the lines under the head and create the collar.

9 Erase your guidelines. Use light brown as a base colour. Add light pink to the nose and mouth, and light green to the eyes.

10 Use a slightly darker tone to create shadows on the head — mainly the ears, along the skin folds and around the eyes. Vary the pressure on your pencil for different degrees of tonal value.

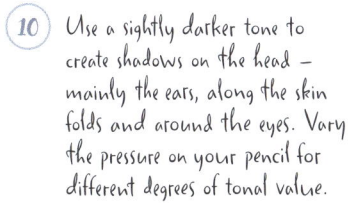

Chow Chow

The Chow Chow is one of the world's oldest dog breeds, earning its place in history as a guarder, hauler, hunter and companion to Chinese nobles.

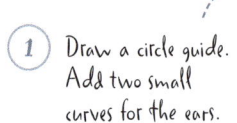

1. Draw a circle guide. Add two small curves for the ears.

2. Add a horizontal line crossing the head, and a vertical line through the top half. Draw a circle directly below the horizontal line for the muzzle.

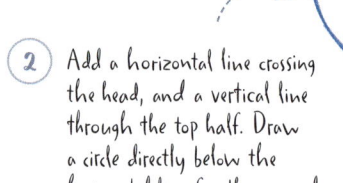

3. Add two smaller circles on each side for the paws.

4. Sketch small, very round eyes, sitting on top of the horizontal guideline and at either side of the vertical line. Lightly sketch the nose.

5. Add a vertical line to split the lower section of the nose in half. Draw two lines that curve back to each side of the muzzle guidelines for the mouth. Draw the ears, adding short strokes in the centre for depth.

6 Draw the rest of the head, using short strokes to create fuzzy fur. Add the tongue and lower jaw.

7 Draw a line on top of the nose to show the skin folds, and add detail to the paws.

8 Erase your guidelines. Add detail to the face. Use small strokes for the eyebrows and under the mouth to create fur.

9 Add light orange as a base colour.

10 Use a slightly darker value to create shadows on the head – mainly the ears and around the eyes. Colour the eyes brown, the nose grey and the tongue this breed's characteristic blue black.

Dogs at rest

Front view:
Body

Now that you have mastered facial features, it is time to
perfect your pooch's body using these ten simple steps.
This front view is the classic sitting pose.

(1) Draw the guidelines
for the head.

(2) Add a circle for the
top part of the body.

(3) Draw two lines for the
front legs, about as long
as the body circle. Add
two circles for paws.

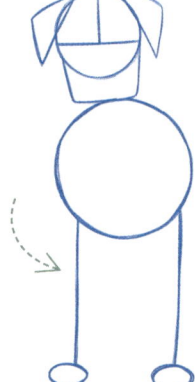

(4) Add another circle
next to each paw
as guides for the
rear paws.

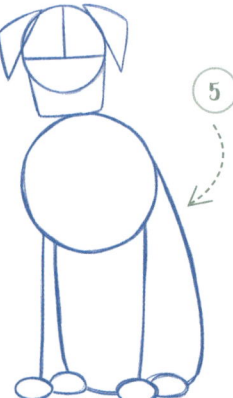

(5) Draw a U-shape
under the circle.
Do not overlap
your leg guidelines.

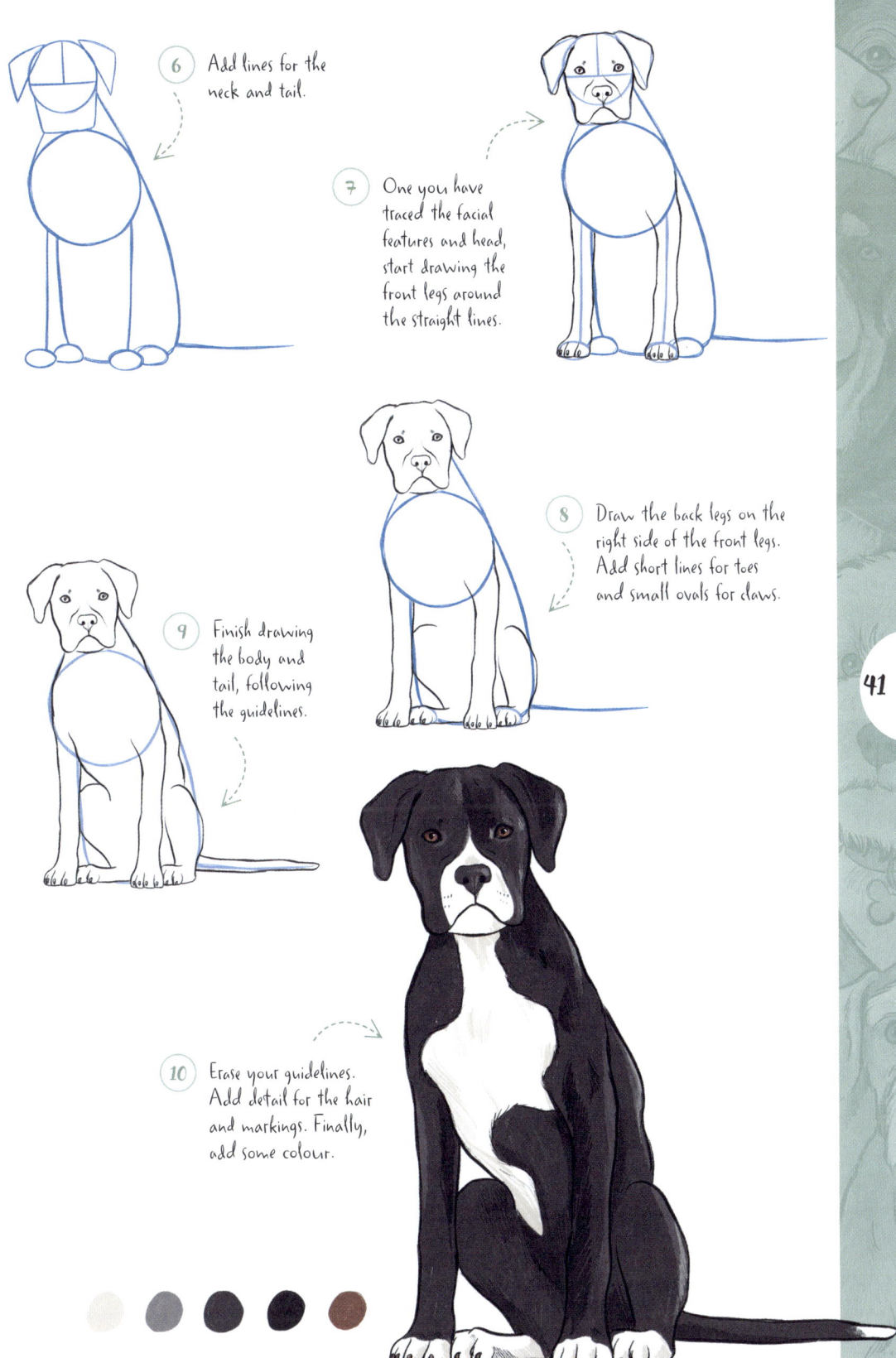

6 Add lines for the neck and tail.

7 One you have traced the facial features and head, start drawing the front legs around the straight lines.

8 Draw the back legs on the right side of the front legs. Add short lines for toes and small ovals for claws.

9 Finish drawing the body and tail, following the guidelines.

10 Erase your guidelines. Add detail for the hair and markings. Finally, add some colour.

Side view:
Body

When drawing the side view of your dog, bear in mind that the legs are always wider at the top, particularly where the thighs are located.

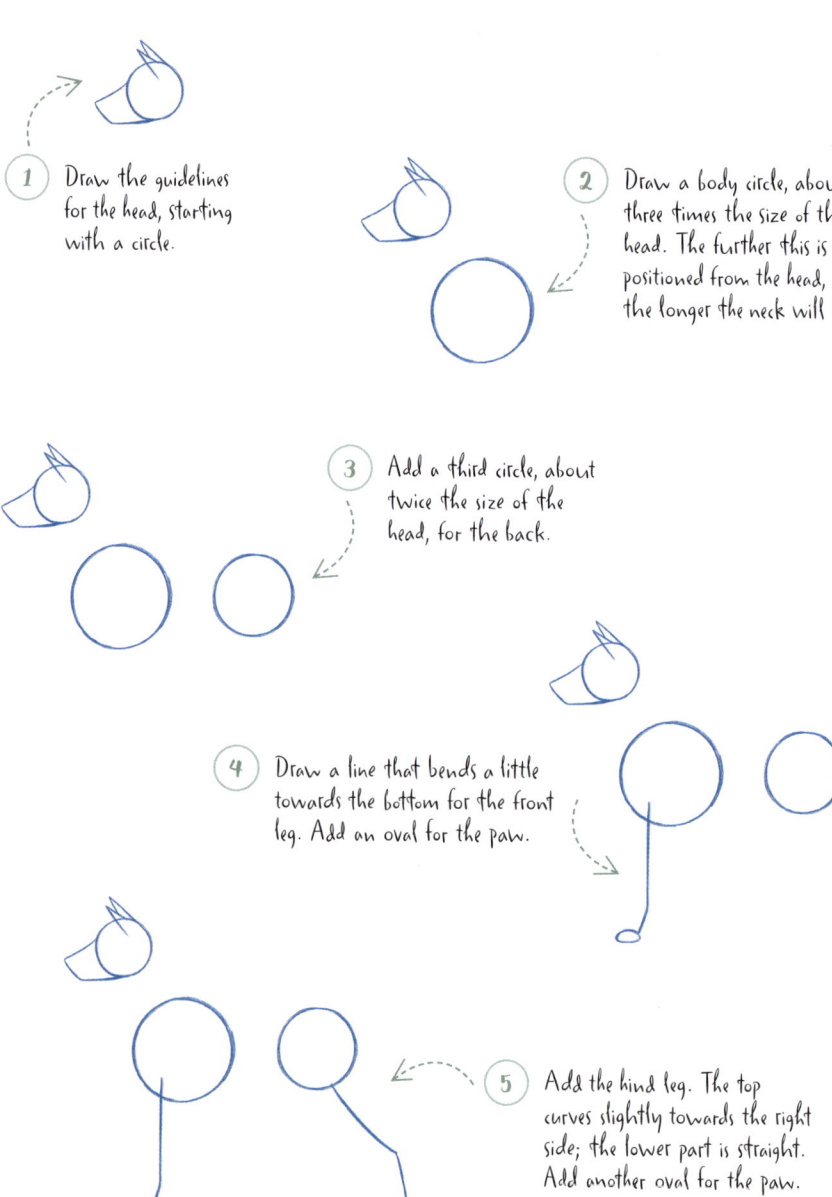

1. Draw the guidelines for the head, starting with a circle.

2. Draw a body circle, about three times the size of the head. The further this is positioned from the head, the longer the neck will be.

3. Add a third circle, about twice the size of the head, for the back.

4. Draw a line that bends a little towards the bottom for the front leg. Add an oval for the paw.

5. Add the hind leg. The top curves slightly towards the right side; the lower part is straight. Add another oval for the paw.

6 Link the shapes together with curved lines, creating the neck, belly and back. Add a twirly line for the tail.

7 Use the initial circle as a guide to draw the head. Draw the front leg, making it wider at the top. Add a few curved lines to create the toes.

8 Draw the back leg, using an angular shape, making it wider at the top. Create the toes with a few curved strokes.

9 Draw the body and tail.

10 Erase your guidelines. Add the remaining legs with a few lines parallel to the existing legs. Add some colour.

German Shepherd

German Shepherds are distinctive with the 'black mask' on their face and the 'saddle' or 'blanket' on their back. Use longer strokes for shaggier fur.

1 Draw a circle guide, adding a horizontal line across the centre and a vertical line through the top half.

2 Draw a small oval on the lower part of the head. Add two long, triangular shapes as guides for ears. Add a U-shape for the chest.

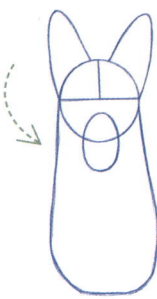

3 Draw a slanted U-shape to the lower right for the body. Add a tail guideline and two lines for the front legs.

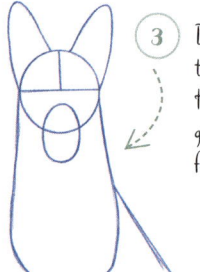

4 Add two shapes for the hind paws. Sketch the eyes, using the guidelines to position them. Draw a tiny reflection circle inside each eye, then a slightly bigger dot for the pupils.

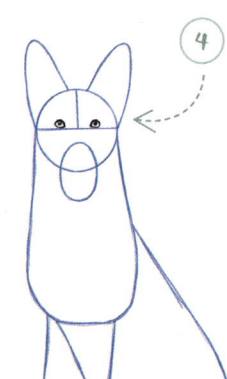

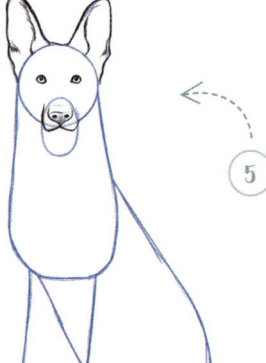

5 Add the nose and nostrils. Draw two curved lines under the nose to create the top lips. Follow the guidelines for the edges of the ears. Add quick, short strokes for the fur inside the ears.

44

6 Draw a U-shape for the tongue, adding the lower jaw around it. Sketch the front legs around the guidelines, adding curved lines for the toes.

7 Draw the rest of the body, hind legs and tail, using quick, short strokes for a furry texture.

8 Erase your guidelines. Add small strokes around the body to resemble fur.

9 Add a light brown base colour. Use darker brown for the eyes and pink for the tongue.

10 Add black to the muzzle, around the eyes, side of the neck, back and top of the tail.

45

Bulldog

When drawing your Bulldog, keep the legs characteristically short. Some Bulldogs are more wrinkly than others, so feel free to add more lines if you like.

(1) Draw a circle guide, with two curved, intersecting lines inside.

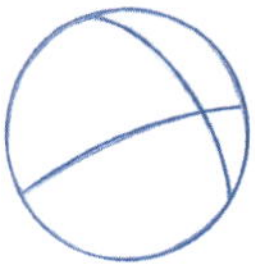

(2) Draw two short, curved lines for the ears and an angled shape for the muzzle.

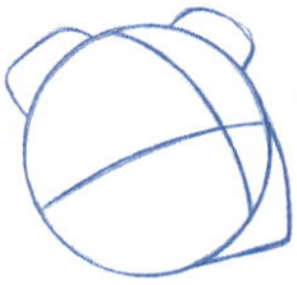

(3) Draw two circles as body guides. The head should overlap the larger circle.

(4) Connect the circles with two curved lines. Draw four short lines as leg guides, bent to indicate the joints.

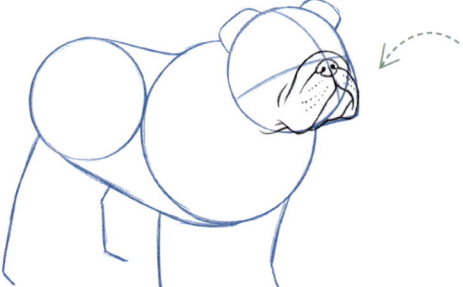

(5) Draw the nose, adding the nostrils. Add a small line to split the bottom of the nose, a short, curved line on either side and a longer curved line for the skin fold above it. Add the floppy top lip, starting under the nose and splitting into two. Add lines around the muzzle for loose skin detail.

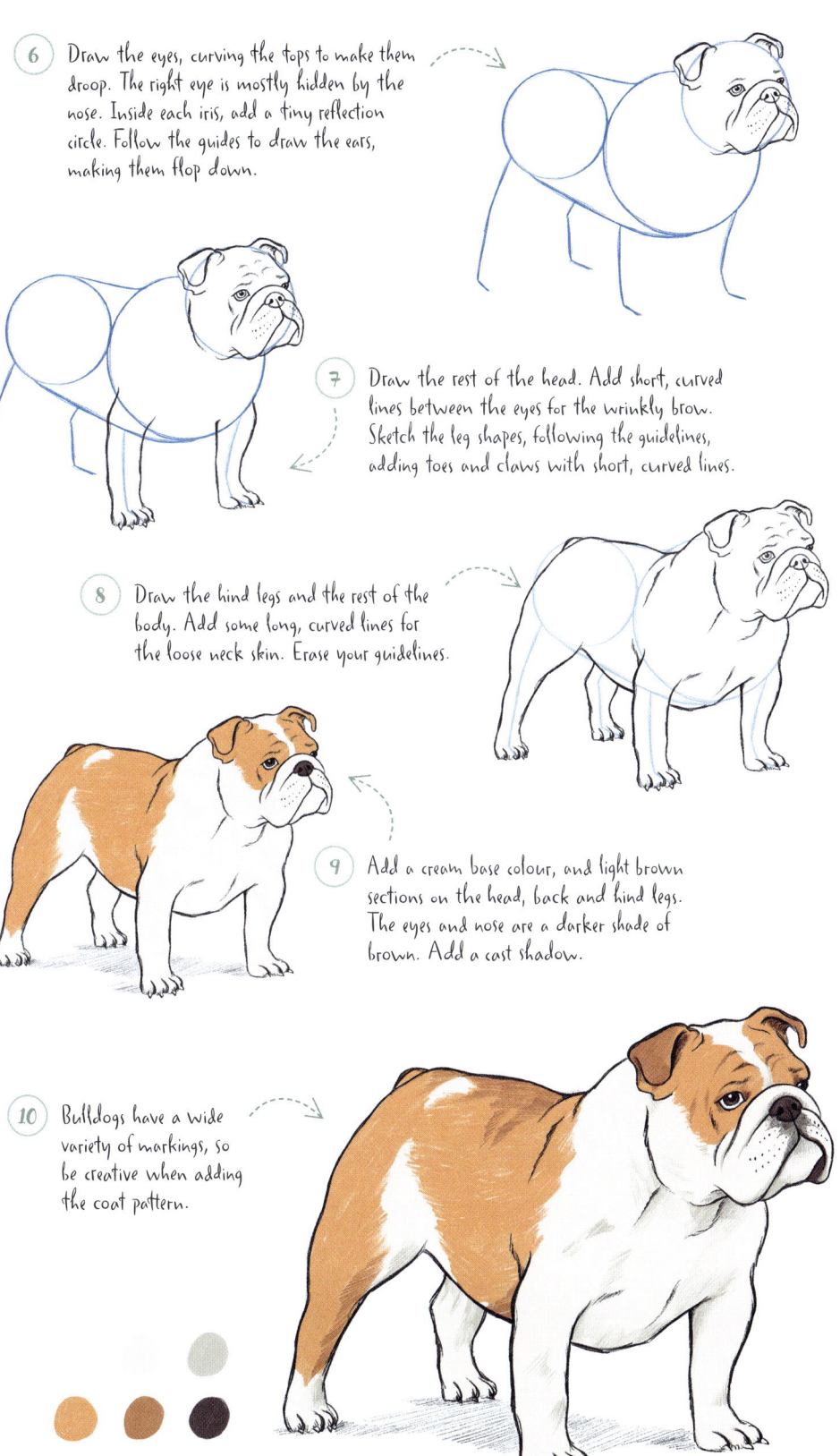

6 Draw the eyes, curving the tops to make them droop. The right eye is mostly hidden by the nose. Inside each iris, add a tiny reflection circle. Follow the guides to draw the ears, making them flop down.

7 Draw the rest of the head. Add short, curved lines between the eyes for the wrinkly brow. Sketch the leg shapes, following the guidelines, adding toes and claws with short, curved lines.

8 Draw the hind legs and the rest of the body. Add some long, curved lines for the loose neck skin. Erase your guidelines.

9 Add a cream base colour, and light brown sections on the head, back and hind legs. The eyes and nose are a darker shade of brown. Add a cast shadow.

10 Bulldogs have a wide variety of markings, so be creative when adding the coat pattern.

French Bulldog

French Bulldogs resemble Bulldogs in miniature, except for their distinctive bat-like ears. They have different types of coats, so you can shade yours however you like.

① Draw a circle guide, adding a horizontal line across the centre and a vertical line through the top half.

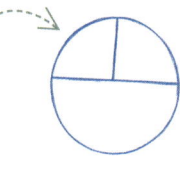

② Draw a small circle on the bottom half and two arcs for the ears.

③ Draw a larger circle as a guide for the front of the body, without overlapping the head, and a smaller circle for the back section.

④ Draw two small lines for the neck and longer lines to connect the two bigger circles. Draw two short, vertical lines as front leg guides, bent to indicate the feet, and a bent hind leg.

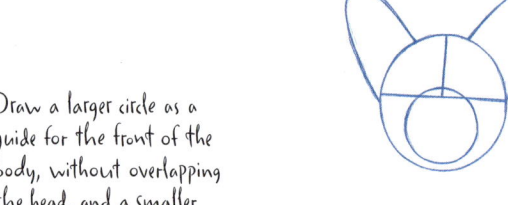

⑤ Sketch the eyes as two small circles with pointed corners. Add eyelids and wrinkle lines. Sketch a small oval for the nose, draw a C-shape facing down and accentuate the ends for the nostrils. Add a short, vertical line to split the nose in half. Draw two curved lines on each side for the upper lips.

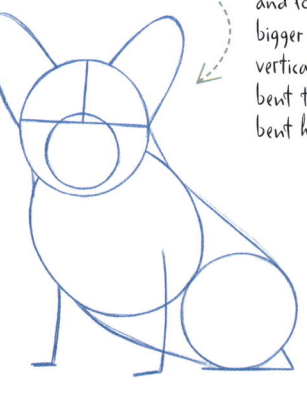

48

6 Draw a curved line over the nose for the folded skin and add the chin. Draw the ears, using wavy lines on the sides. Add short strokes for the hair and inner ear structure.

7 Draw the front legs, making them wider at the tops. Add short lines to separate the toes and add claws.

8 Sketch the hind leg and draw the rest of the body. Erase your guidelines.

9 Start with a light brown base colour. Use green for the eyes, brown for the nose and around the eyes, and pink for inside the ears.

10 To create shadows, use a dark value on the muzzle, around the eyes and on the ears, and a medium value for the rest of the body.

Yorkshire Terrier

Small in size but big in personality, Yorkies can have a variety of coat colours. The longer you draw your strokes, the longer the fur will appear.

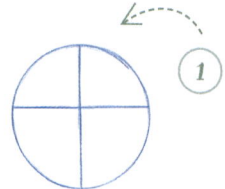

1. Draw a circle guide with two intersecting lines.

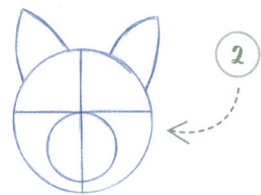

2. Draw a smaller circle for the muzzle guide and two small, triangular arcs for ears.

3. Trace a loaf-like body shape, and add two lines for the front legs.

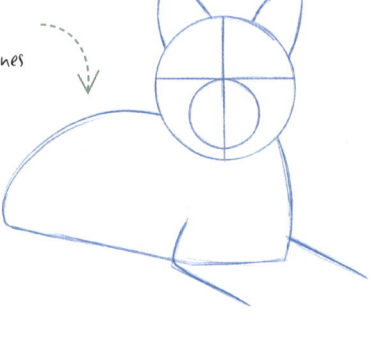

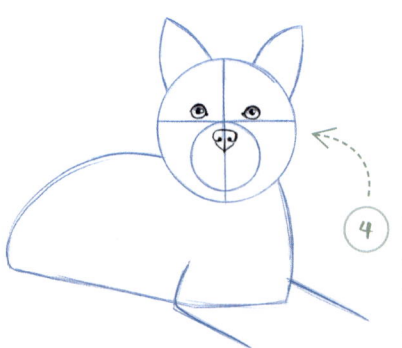

4. Draw the eyes, adding a tiny reflection circle to the side of each eye and bigger central dots for the pupils. Draw a pointed nose along the vertical line, adding two smaller circles for nostrils.

5. Draw the top of the muzzle, using quick, short strokes to represent fur. The fur at the top should almost cover the eyes. The muzzle should be wider than the circle guide.

6 Draw a few quick, short strokes along the triangular ear shapes.

7 Draw quick, short strokes around the circle guide to create the furry head. Follow the guidelines and use quick, short strokes to shape the front legs.

8 Add a few strokes above the eyes for more texture. Use the initial loaf-like shape as a guide to draw the body, using quick, short strokes.

9 Erase your guidelines. For a standard Yorkie, use medium brown for the head and front legs.

10 Add some darker shading to the coat, using values that vary from medium to dark throughout the body to emphasize the shadows and highlights.

Cockapoo

Cockapoos are the highly affectionate, adorable cross between the Cocker Spaniel and the Poodle. This curly haired companion looks well-rested and ready to play.

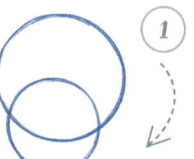

1. Draw a circle guide. Add a smaller, overlapping circle on the lower part as a muzzle guide.

2. Draw a vertical line through the head circle, slightly inclined to the right, and a curved line within the muzzle. Draw two long arcs as guides for the ears.

3. Add a triangular body shape under the head, with two U-shapes beneath it for the front legs.

4. Draw a curve on the right side, linking the chest to the ear, and add a little arc below the left ear for the hind leg.

5. Add guide details for the toy and collar. Draw the nose in the centre of the muzzle guideline, shading in two small circles for nostrils. Use short strokes to create the fur around the muzzle and a tuft of longer hair between the eyes.

6 Draw two small, round balls for the eyes, adding tiny reflection circles to the sides and bigger dots for pupils. Use short strokes to draw the rest of the head.

7 Make quick, short strokes along the side arcs for the furry ears, and along the chin.

8 Add detail to the collar and toy.

9 Follow the guides to draw the body, using quick, short strokes. Erase your guidelines.

10 Colour the collar and toy, then add a pale brown base colour. Use darker tones around the eyes, nose, ears, back and legs. Colour the eyes medium brown and the nose dark brown.

Rottweiler

This Rottweiler is ready and eager to play ball! Give him an extra-shiny coat by adding darker values to parts of his body.

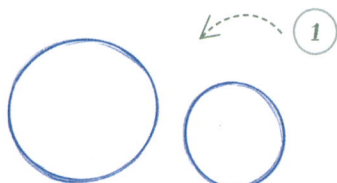

1 For the body guides, draw a large circle on the left with a smaller circle beside it.

2 Draw an overlapping, smaller rectangular head shape with rounded corners.

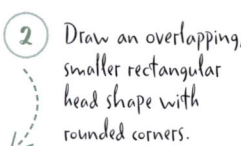

3 Draw two intersecting lines inside the head. Add a small oval on the lower part and triangular shapes on each side as guides for the muzzle and ears.

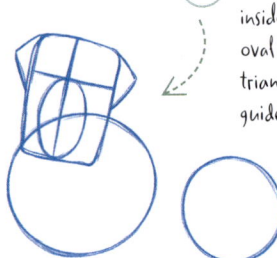

54

4 Draw two guides for the legs below each circle, indicating the joints, and adding circles for paws. Draw the tennis ball between the front paws and add the tail.

5 Link the circles together for the back and belly. Draw football-shaped eyes, using the guides for placement. Add a tiny C-shape inside each eye to represent the pupil and reflection. Draw the nose, adding a curved line above it to show a skin fold.

6 Complete the muzzle. The mouth consists of a wavy line under the nose. Draw the tongue, loose skin and chin using a series of curved lines. Draw the ears, making the shapes curvier.

7 Draw the front legs, feet and ball. Add curved lines for the toes.

8 Draw the hind legs and tail. Erase your guidelines.

9 Colour the head, body, legs and tail dark grey, with light brown patches on the muzzle, cheeks, eyebrows, paws and chest.

10 Add an orange brown to the eyes, pink to the tongue, dark brown to the nose and grey to the claws. Add shading throughout.

Dachshund

This slick, short-haired Dachshund is created using smooth lines for the body. For a long-haired coat, use quick, short strokes.

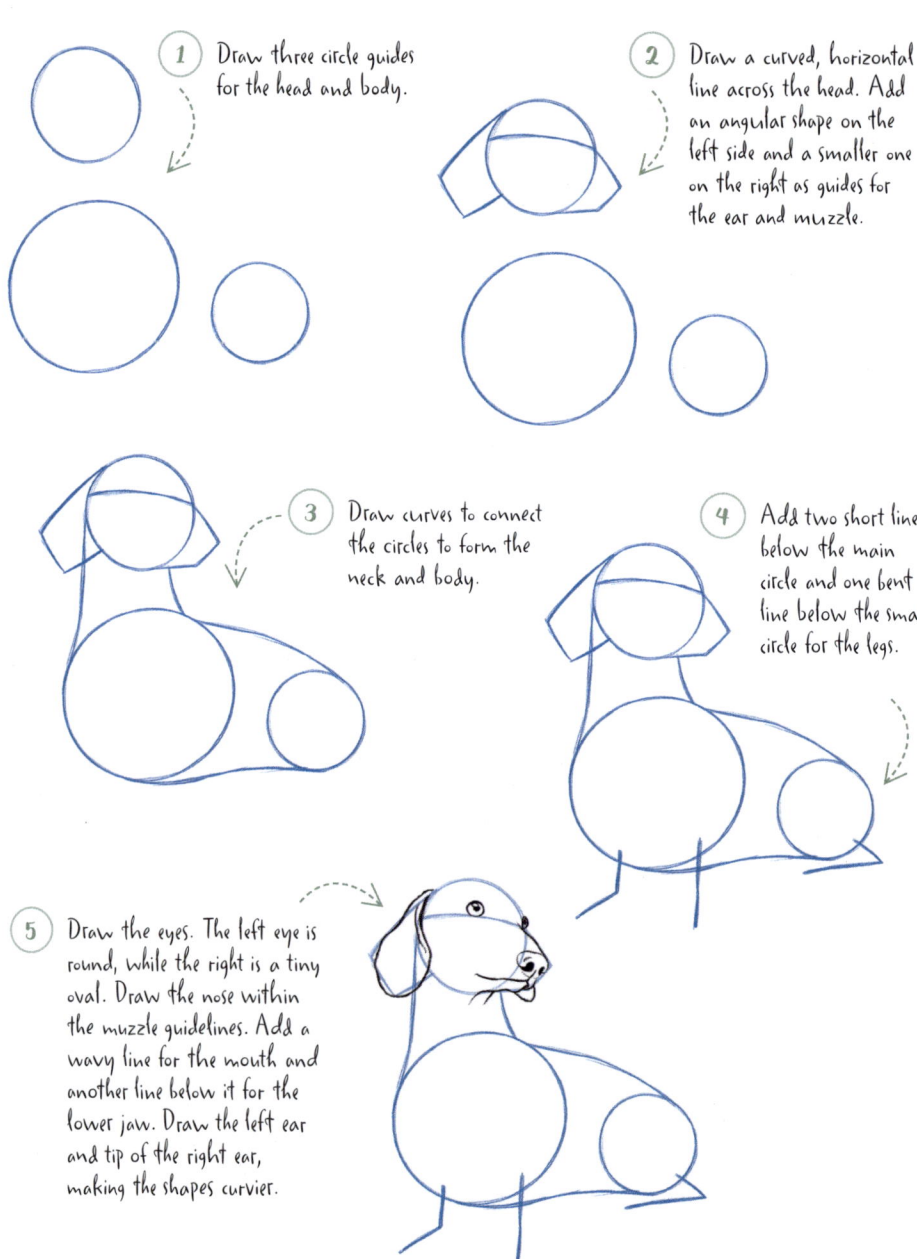

1 Draw three circle guides for the head and body.

2 Draw a curved, horizontal line across the head. Add an angular shape on the left side and a smaller one on the right as guides for the ear and muzzle.

3 Draw curves to connect the circles to form the neck and body.

4 Add two short lines below the main circle and one bent line below the small circle for the legs.

5 Draw the eyes. The left eye is round, while the right is a tiny oval. Draw the nose within the muzzle guidelines. Add a wavy line for the mouth and another line below it for the lower jaw. Draw the left ear and tip of the right ear, making the shapes curvier.

6 Add a few curved lines along the neck to represent skin folds. Draw the front legs and feet, adding bumps to represent the joints. Draw lines for the toes and nails.

7 Draw the hind leg and the visible portion of the last leg.

8 Use the connecting lines as guides to draw the rest of the body. Erase your guidelines.

9 Use a dark grey for the main coat colour, leaving some spots white. Colour the eyes brown.

10 Finish with defined spots of grey and brown, and add a shadow.

Miniature Schnauzer

Their iconic, bushy beards and eyebrows give Miniature Schnauzers a quirky, human-like expression. Full of personality, this dog is intelligent, inquisitive and extroverted.

① Draw a rectangular guide for the head. Draw a horizontal line one-third of the way down, a vertical line on top and a circle for the muzzle.

② Draw two U-shapes on each side for the ears. Under the head, draw two parallel lines leaning to the bottom left.

③ Draw two sausage-shaped guides for the front legs.

④ Add two round shapes to the left of the front leg to help define the right hind leg.

⑤ Draw small, round eyes, using the guidelines for placement. Sketch the nose, adding two black dots to create nostrils. Draw a short, vertical line to split the nose in half, then add two curved lines on each side to define the upper lip.

6　Use short strokes to draw two thick, arc-like shapes for the bushy eyebrows. Around the head and ears, draw a series of short strokes to represent the fur. Use longer strokes on the lower edge of the rectangle to create the moustache shape.

7　Follow the guides to draw the front legs.

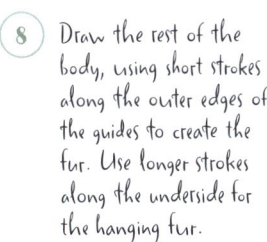

8　Draw the rest of the body, using short strokes along the outer edges of the guides to create the fur. Use longer strokes along the underside for the hanging fur.

59

9　Erase your guidelines. Add a light grey tone to the body, with a very light value for the brows, moustache and beard.

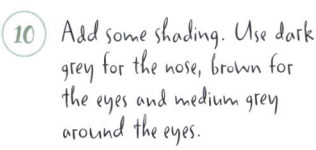

10　Add some shading. Use dark grey for the nose, brown for the eyes and medium grey around the eyes.

Pomeranian

The Pom's profuse double coat stands out, and he has a luxurious ruff around his neck and chest. The longer your strokes are, the shaggier his fur will be.

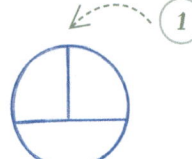

1. Draw a circle guide, adding a horizontal line across the centre and a shorter vertical line through the top half.

2. Draw a small circle for the muzzle guide and two small semicircles for the ears.

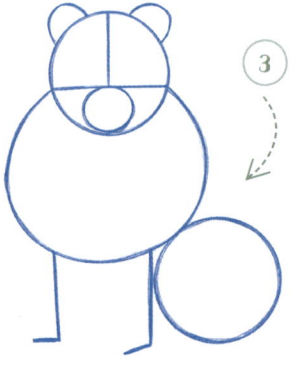

3. Draw a bigger circle for the front of the body, making sure the head circle overlaps it. Draw a smaller circle for the back of the body. Add two short lines with bent feet as front leg guides.

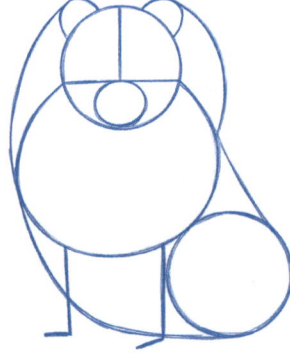

4. Draw two curves connecting the two body circles and two curves around the head, linking the top of the ears to the middle of the larger body circle.

5. Draw the eyes, using the guidelines for placement. Draw the nose within the muzzle.

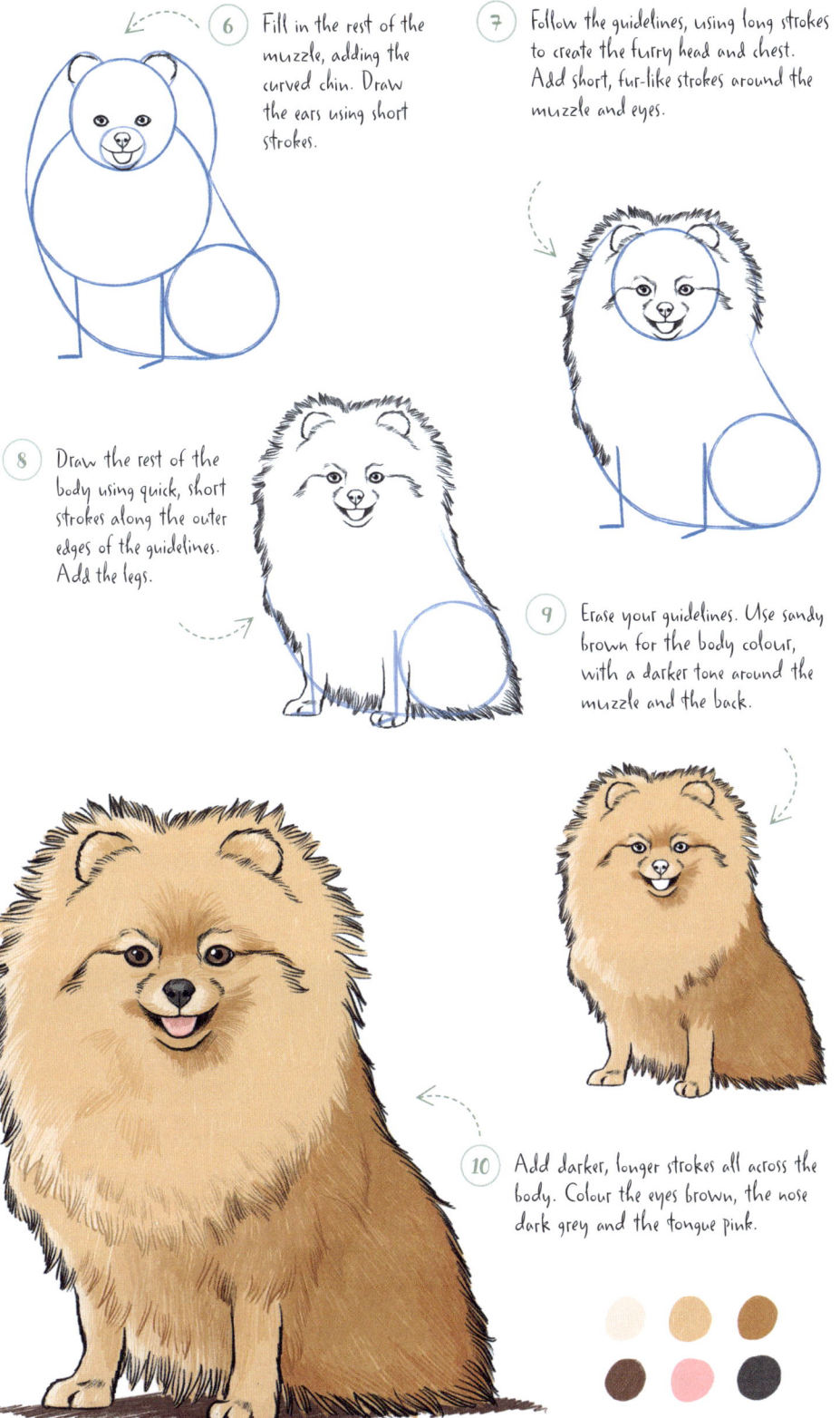

6 Fill in the rest of the muzzle, adding the curved chin. Draw the ears using short strokes.

7 Follow the guidelines, using long strokes to create the furry head and chest. Add short, fur-like strokes around the muzzle and eyes.

8 Draw the rest of the body using quick, short strokes along the outer edges of the guidelines. Add the legs.

9 Erase your guidelines. Use sandy brown for the body colour, with a darker tone around the muzzle and the back.

10 Add darker, longer strokes all across the body. Colour the eyes brown, the nose dark grey and the tongue pink.

Chihuahua

A small dog with a big attitude, the Chihuahua is recognized by its short, shiny coat and ruff of thick, longer hair on its neck and ears.

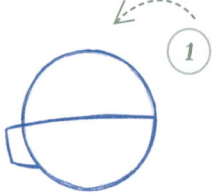

1 Draw a circle guide. Add a horizontal line across the centre and a rectangular shape on the left for the muzzle.

2 Draw a small, curved shape for the bottom of the muzzle and two small triangles as ear guides; the right ear should be larger than the left.

3 Draw a similar-sized circle as a guide for the front of the body, making sure the head overlaps it. Draw a smaller horizontal oval directly under it for the back of the body.

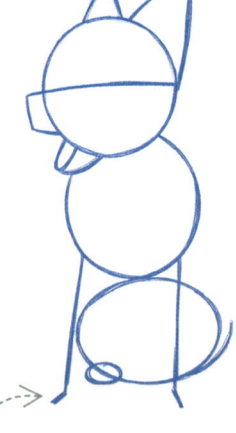

4 Add two straight lines for the front legs. Draw a small curve on the lower right side of the oval for the tail and a small circle beside the front leg for the hind paw.

5 Draw the eyes, with the right eye under the guideline and the barely visible left eye over it. Draw the nose within the top muzzle guideline.

6 Draw the mouth and chin.

7 Use quick, short strokes around the head, and draw the ears. Use short strokes to trace the front legs around the guidelines, and longer strokes for the fur on the back of the head.

8 Draw the rest of the body, using quick, short strokes. Add thinner lines for coat markings. Draw two eyebrow shapes and some lines around the muzzle and on the front and belly.

9 Erase your guidelines. Add dark grey colouring, with light brown and white accents.

10 Colour the eyes brown, and the inside of the ears and tongue dark pink.

Bernese Mountain Dog

Characteristically tricoloured, the long-haired Bernese Mountain Dog is an extremely versatile working dog, bred to herd cattle in the farmlands of Switzerland.

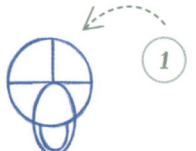

1 Draw a circle guide, adding a horizontal line across the centre and a shorter vertical line through the top half. Draw an oval, overlapping the head circle, for the muzzle, and a U-shaped tongue.

2 Add two long, floppy shapes for the ears.

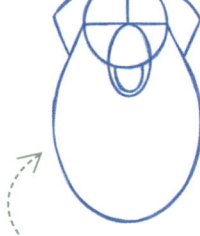

3 Add a U-shape for the top part of the body.

4 Draw another shape for the lower part of the body. Add an oval paw on the bottom right, and two lines for the legs, starting halfway down the body.

5 Draw the eyes, using the guidelines for placement. Add a tiny reflection circle inside each eye and a slightly bigger dot for the pupils. Draw the nose inside the muzzle.

6 Draw two curves under the nose for the top lips and use the U-shape to draw the tongue. Draw the ears, giving them a wavy outline, with long strokes for the fur.

7 Draw lines around the muzzle to create the lower jaw. Use the guidelines to draw the front legs, adding a few curved lines for toes.

8 Follow the guides, using quick strokes to draw the rest of the furry body.

9 Erase your guidelines. Add some small strokes to prepare your markings. Colour the body jet black, with tan patches and white markings on the chest, between the eyes and on the feet.

10 Add darker shading to give the coat a silky look, pink for the tongue and brown tones for the eyes and mouth.

Pug

These cute and cuddly little dogs have roly-poly rolls of skin and stumpy, chunky bodies. They have a stubborn, playful streak, too.

1 Draw a circle guide, with two curved, intersecting lines inside.

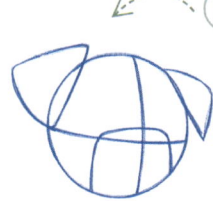

2 Draw a square-shaped muzzle guide and two triangular shapes for the ears.

3 Draw a triangular shape for the body.

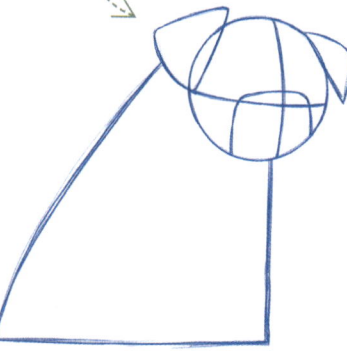

4 Add guidelines across the triangular shape for the legs and a small circle for the tail.

5 Draw the eyes. Where the two guidelines intersect, draw an oval for the nose with lines that curl inwards for the nostrils. Add the mouth, coming down from the nose, splitting in two and curling up. Add the lips and chin. Draw the ears, rounding the corners.

6　Draw the rest of the head and back, using quick, short strokes to represent fur. Add curves around the neck and back to represent loose skin folds.

7　Use quick, short strokes to draw the rest of the body and legs, with curved lines for the toes.

8　Erase your guidelines. Add some shading to give your drawing dimension.

9　Use beige as a base colour. Darken the area around the eyes and the muzzle.

10　Add dark brown to the ears, and shading around the skin folds and tail.

Saint Bernard

These huge dogs are strong and muscular, with a powerful head and intelligent expression. They make great companions – if you do not mind a little drool!

1 Draw a circle guide. Add an oval shape for the muzzle.

2 Add two triangular shapes as ear guides (only the tip of the left ear is visible). Add a neck shape.

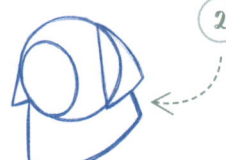

3 Add a U-shape for the top of the body. Draw a backwards L-shape on the lower right side for the lower body and two lines for the front legs. Add guidelines to the face to help position the features.

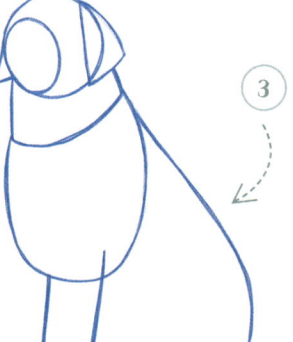

4 Add two ovals for the hind leg and tail. Across the muzzle, draw an upside-down Y-shape. Under the head circle, add a U-shape for the lower jaw.

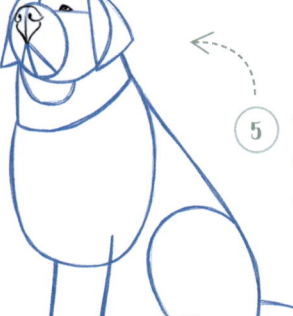

5 Draw the right eye, using the guidelines for placement. Add the nose.

6 From the bottom of the nose, add two diagonal lines to the edge of the muzzle oval. Add the chin along the U-shape. Draw the ears, using quick, short strokes to resemble fur. Follow the guidelines to draw the front legs and hind leg, adding curves for the toes.

7 Use short strokes to follow the neck guide, giving it a furry edge below the right ear.

8 Draw the rest of the body and tail, using quick, short strokes for a furry texture. Erase your guidelines.

9 Add light beige to the chest, neck, noseband, legs and tail. Use bright brown for the rest of the body.

10 Add some darker shading to your drawing. Use brown for the eyes and pink for the tongue.

Australian Shepherd

You can experiment with colour when drawing these wonderful dogs, who come in blue merle, red merle, red, tricolour and black.

1. Draw a circle guide. Add a straight line across and an oval on the lower half as a muzzle guide.

2. Add two small, pointy shapes for ears. Trace two small, vertical lines along the horizontal line to help position the eyes.

3. Trace a loaf-like shape for the body. Add two lines with circles for the front legs and paws.

4. On the left side of the body, sketch a C-shape for the back. Add an oval tail.

5. Draw the eyes, adding a tiny reflection circle and a bigger dot for the pupils. Add the nose towards the top left of the muzzle guide. Add two smaller circles for nostrils, and a small line to split the bottom of the nose.

6 For the mouth, split the line at the bottom of the nose into two curves. Follow the circle guide to draw the bottom jaw and chin. Add teeth. Use short strokes to draw the fluffy ears.

7 Draw quick, short strokes along the U-shape for the body. Use guidelines to draw the front legs with short strokes.

8 Use the C-shaped guide to draw the back of the body and tail.

9 Erase your guidelines. Draw some thinner lines for the markings. Colour with a light grey as a base layer, adding darker grey and orange patches.

10 Finalize your drawing with darker tones for the coat. As the coat is a little scruffy, your pencil strokes can show.

German Shorthaired Pointer

The highly energetic German Shorthaired Pointer is one of the world's most accomplished sporting and hunting breeds, and also makes a beloved companion.

1. Draw three circle guides for the head and body, spaced a little apart. Draw a straight, horizontal line across the top circle.

2. Add a small muzzle shape on the right side of the head and a U-shape on the left side for the ear.

72

3. Draw two lines under the large circle and three lines to the back circle as guides for the legs and tail.

4. Finalize your guidelines by adding lines to link the shapes.

5. Draw the eye on the horizontal guideline. Add a tiny reflection circle and a slightly bigger dot for the pupil. Draw the nose at the tip of the muzzle.

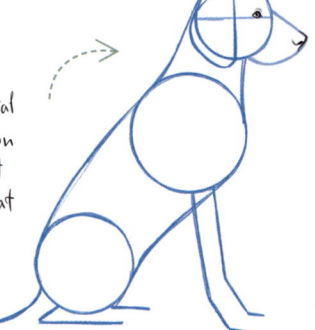

6 Use the guide to draw the ear, giving it structure with wavy strokes. Finish drawing the muzzle and draw the head, following the guidelines.

7 Use the guidelines to draw the front legs, adding curves for the toes. Repeat with the hind legs and tail.

8 Draw the rest of the body, keeping your strokes simple for a smooth effect. Erase your guidelines.

9 Add light beige as a base colour and medium brown for some patches on the head, back and tail.

10 Add little brown spots all over the body, focusing on the back and the front legs to depict the ticked coat.

Chinese Shar-Pei

Shar-Pei are recognizable by their short, bristly coats; characteristic loose, wrinkled skin; and frowning expressions. They are very devoted dogs.

1 Draw a circle guide, adding a horizontal line across the centre and a shorter vertical line through the top half. Add an oval shape, overlapping the head circle, for the muzzle.

2 Draw two small ovals as ear guides, with one crossing the head circle and the other contained within it. Trace a semicircle along the horizontal line to help place the eyes.

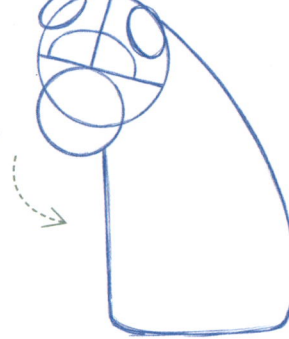

3 Draw a triangular shape as a guide for the body.

4 Add guidelines for the front leg, starting from the top-left corner of the triangular shape, and the hind leg from the bottom-left corner. Add a small curve for the tail.

5 Draw the eyes, using the guidelines for placement. Draw the nose within the muzzle guidelines — the nostrils are very small.

6 Draw the muzzle. Add a line for the mouth coming down from the nose, splitting in two and curling up. Draw another small line for the bottom lip. Draw the ears.

7 Use smooth strokes to draw the rest of the head. Add curved lines on top of the eyes and around the muzzle for skin folds.

8 Use the guidelines to draw the legs, using quick, smooth strokes. Add a simple, curved tail shape.

9 Add lots of crossing lines throughout the body to create a wrinkled effect. Erase your guidelines.

10 Add a light brown base colour. Darken the ears, the back area and along the skin folds.

Dogs in motion

Doberman Pinscher

Doberman Pinschers were originally bred as guard dogs, but this smart, short-haired breed performs well in police work and canine sports, and as family guardians.

1 Draw three circles as guides for the body and head.

2 Draw a horizontal line inside the head and a small, rectangular shape for the muzzle guide. Add a triangle for the ear.

3 Draw a series of lines to connect the circles to form the body. Add a rectangular collar shape.

4 Draw a line under each circle as a guide for the legs, bent to indicate the joints.

5 Add the other legs and a curved line for the tail.

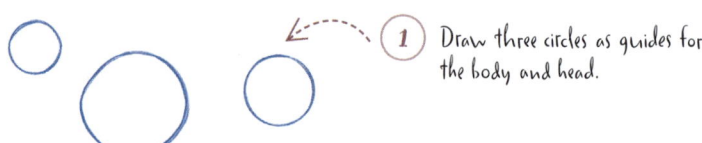
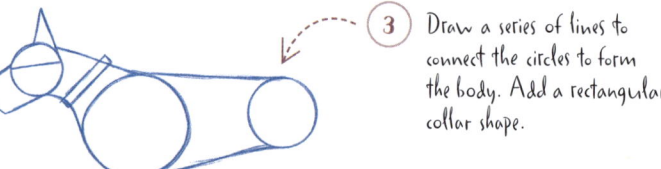
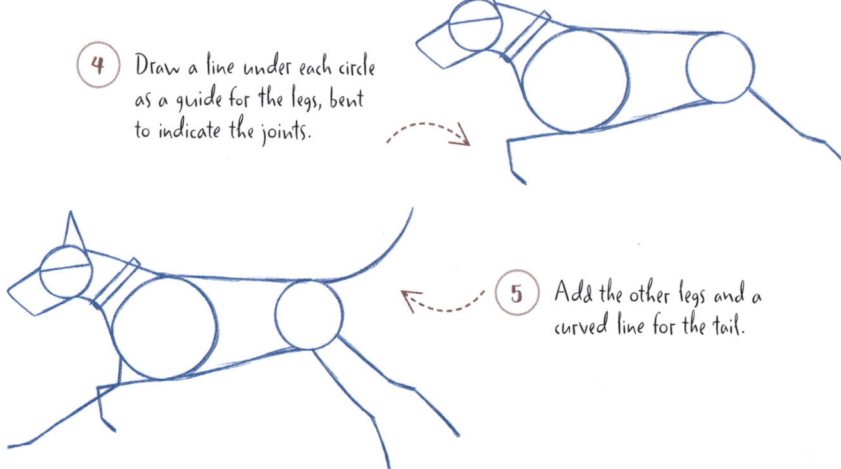

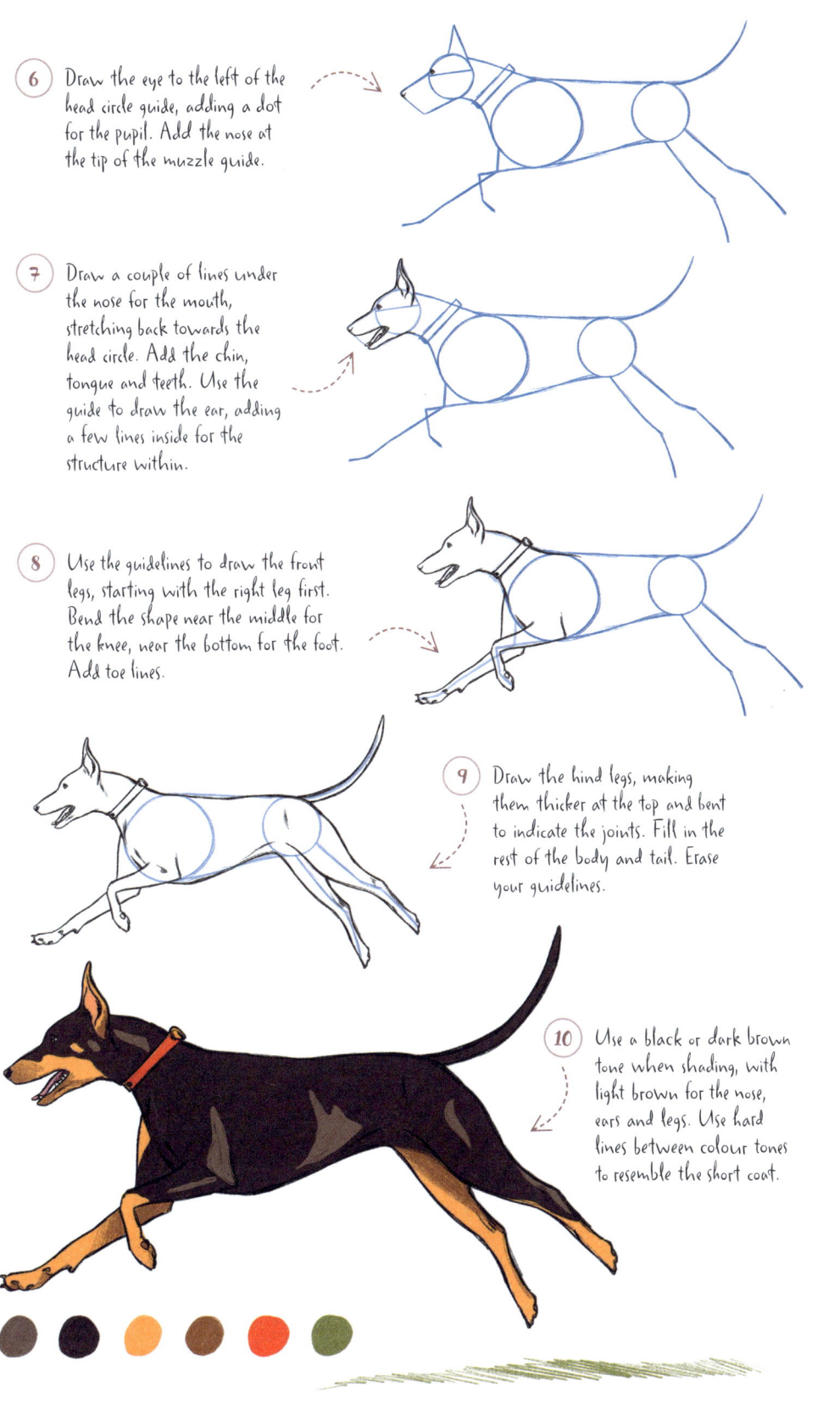

6 Draw the eye to the left of the head circle guide, adding a dot for the pupil. Add the nose at the tip of the muzzle guide.

7 Draw a couple of lines under the nose for the mouth, stretching back towards the head circle. Add the chin, tongue and teeth. Use the guide to draw the ear, adding a few lines inside for the structure within.

8 Use the guidelines to draw the front legs, starting with the right leg first. Bend the shape near the middle for the knee, near the bottom for the foot. Add toe lines.

9 Draw the hind legs, making them thicker at the top and bent to indicate the joints. Fill in the rest of the body and tail. Erase your guidelines.

10 Use a black or dark brown tone when shading, with light brown for the nose, ears and legs. Use hard lines between colour tones to resemble the short coat.

Boxer

Square-jawed, muscular Boxer dogs have smooth, shiny coats,
so try to shade evenly and smoothly to achieve this sleek look.

(1) Draw three circles for
the body and head. On
the left-hand circle, add
a horizontal line across
the centre and a shorter
vertical line through the
top half.

(2) Draw a small circle for the
muzzle and a large triangle for
the ear. Link the three circles
together with curved lines.

(3) Add the front legs, hind
leg and a curved tail.

(4) Draw oval eyes. Add a
tiny highlight circle inside
each eye and a larger
pupil. Draw an oval nose,
adding a small line at the
bottom and nostril circles.

(5) Draw a line starting under the nose, curving
right, and ending on the lower edge of the
initial circle. Complete the other side for the
droopy top lip. Add a curve under the mouth
and lines on top of the nose for skin folds.

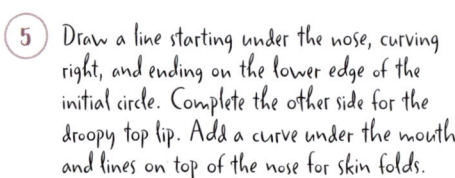

6 Draw the ear with a few quick, short strokes. Draw the rest of the head, making the top part flatter and left side narrower. Draw the front legs, bending the shape to create joints. Add tiny triangles for claws.

7 Draw the hind leg, making the top part wider, curving the middle section to show muscle structure, and adding toe lines and claws.

8 Darken the initial guides to draw the body, adding a few lines to indicate the left hind leg. Fill in the pointy tail. Erase your guidelines.

9 Use dark grey for the muzzle and around the eyes, and medium brown for the rest of the body, leaving a section on the nose and bottom of the legs white.

10 Colour the nose black, the ears dark brown and the eyes light brown. Add shading under the ear, throat, chest and ground to show shadow.

Shih Tzu

The name Shih Tzu means 'little lion', but there's
nothing fierce about this adorably fluffy dog.

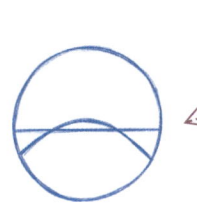

1. Draw a circle guide. Add a
   straight horizontal line and
   an overlapping curve.

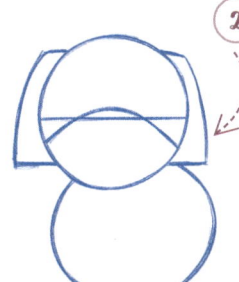

2. Draw two rectangular
   shapes for ears. Draw a
   similar-sized circle for
   the body, with the
   head overlapping.

3. Draw a slightly smaller,
   backwards C-shape for
   the back of the body.

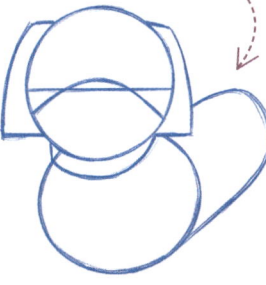

4. Draw vertical guidelines for
   the front legs and one hind
   leg, and circular feet. Add a
   curved line between the back
   and head for the tail guide.

5. Draw a small oval nose along the horizontal
   line, curving the sides inwards to form nostrils.
   Add a small dividing line between them.
   Sketch the eyeballs as two small circles,
   keeping them open at the bottom.

6 Use quick, short strokes over the top of the nose for the fuzzy fur and longer strokes for sides of the face.

7 Follow the guides to draw the furry ears with long strokes. Use shorter strokes for the front and hind legs.

8 Draw the rest of the body, using quick, short strokes. Finish with longer strokes on the fluffy tail.

9 Erase your guidelines and add lines around the eyes, chin and legs to create a furry effect. Add beige and light brown tones to the body.

10 Use a dark value around the eyes and ears, but leave the forehead and muzzle light. The fur radiates around the eyes but is vertical on the ears. Add a cast shadow.

Weimaraner

The Weimaraner's coat is short, smooth and solid-coloured,
ranging from mouse grey to silver grey. While drawing, use very
smooth lines to achieve a sleek look.

1 Draw a circle guide. Add a
horizontal line a third of the
way down and a muzzle
shape on the left.

2 Draw a triangular
shape for the ear.

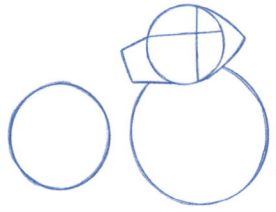

3 Draw two circles for the body.
The left circle should be
slightly smaller.

4 Draw two long, vertical lines
under each circle as leg guides.
Bend the lines near the bottom
of the hind legs to indicate
joints, and for the feet.

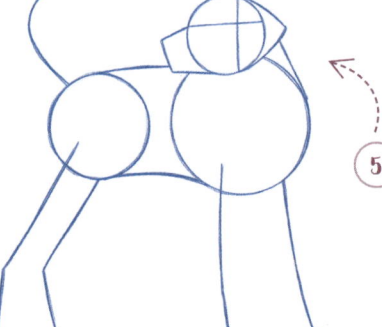

5 Draw lines to connect the two
body circles. Add a small line
below the ear for the neck.
Draw a long, curved tail.

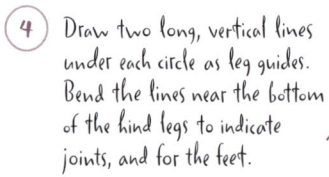

6 Sketch two small circles for the eyes. The left eye should be thinner and smaller because of the way the head is turned. Draw the nose at the tip of the muzzle, and the ear.

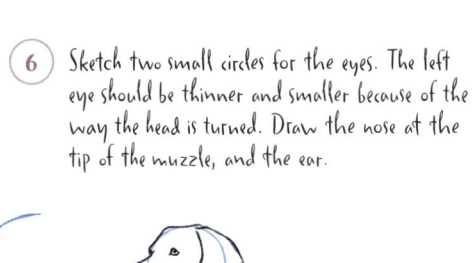

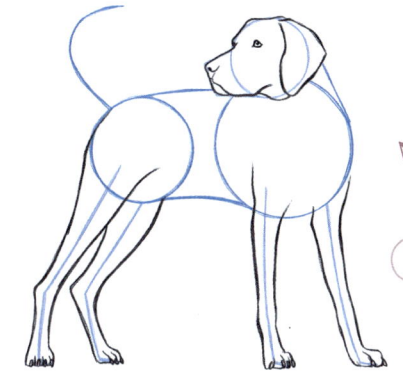

7 Use the guides to draw the rest of the head, making the shape blockier. Fill in the legs, adding toes and claws.

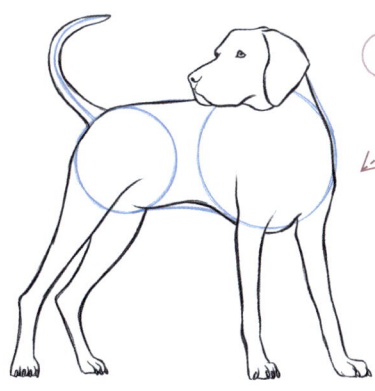

8 Darken the remaining guidelines to draw the rest of the body, making the lines more curved for a more organic feel. Fill in the pointy tail.

9 Erase your guidelines and add a collar.

10 Start with a light beige base, then add some shading with light-brown tones. Add some green lines around the paws to make your dog stand on grass.

Whippet

The sleek, streamlined, sweet-faced Whippet is lightning fast. Highly energetic, it loves nothing more than springing around a park.

1. Draw three circles as guides for the head and body. Make the head circle (a) one-quarter the size of the central body circle (b), leaving space for the long neck.

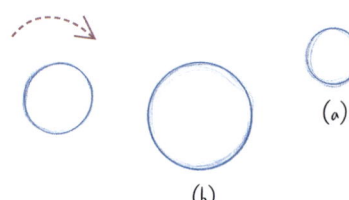

2. Link the three circles together with straight lines.

3. Under the left and middle circles, draw two long lines for the legs. Bend them in the middle and add small circles to indicate the joints.

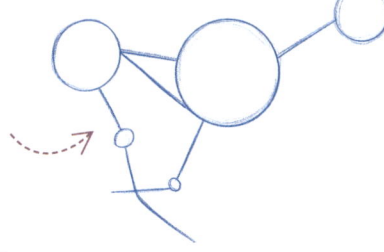

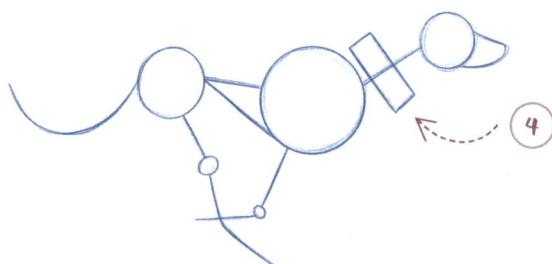

4. Draw a small arc as a muzzle guide, about the same width as the head. Add a rectangle towards the bottom of the neck line and a curved tail.

5. Draw two curved lines to connect the head to the body, creating a guide for the neck and back.

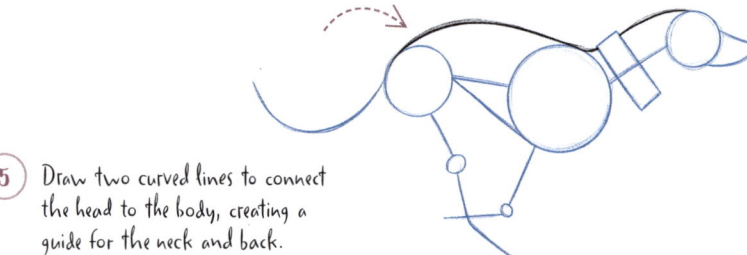

6 Draw a small, pointed circle for the eye and add a dot for the pupil. Draw a dark, triangular nose at the tip of the muzzle, leaving a tiny, angled line white for the nostril. Complete the rest of the muzzle. Add a small line inside the ear for the skin creases. Draw the collar.

7 Sketch the first hind leg around the guidelines. It should be widest at the top. Draw the paw, using short, curved lines for the toes. Add guidelines for the other two legs and fill in the tail.

8 Draw the other legs the same way, adding toes at the bottom with curved lines. Follow the guides to complete the chest and belly.

9 Erase your guidelines. Add shading to give dimension to your drawing.

10 For a simple grey coat, use a medium value all over the body, with a slightly lighter value around the neck and shoulder to make the coat shiny. Add green to the eye and red to the collar. Add a cast shadow.

Poodle

This elegant, proud and intelligent poodle – with long ears, a pompom tail
and distinctive curly coat – is born to be best in show.

1 Draw two circles
as guides for the
head and body.

2 Draw a small rectangle for the
back of the body, and four
straight lines for legs.

3 Draw a horizontal oval
intersecting the top of the
head circle, and two long,
curved lines on either side
as ear guides.

4 Draw a small circle for the tail
and four circles at the bottom
of the legs.

5 Shade a small circle for each
eye, adding a tiny reflection
circle. Draw the nose, adding
nostrils on each side.

6 Follow the path of the curved oval above the head, using short, curved lines on top and above the eyes to resemble fluffy fur. Continue around the ear guides.

7 Continue using short, curved lines to add fur to the four small circles on the ankles, widening the shapes as you go. Use the straight lines as guides to draw the legs. Add toes and nails.

8 Add short markings to the tail. Finish tracing the body, using the larger circle as a guide to add fluffy fur to the chest. Erase your guidelines.

9 Add light beige as a base colour, green for the eyes and brown for the nose.

10 Add some shading to give the poodle more dimension and volume. Finish with a cast shadow.

Basset Hound

These smart, easygoing dogs are instantly recognizable by
their long, smooth-haired bodies; short, crooked legs;
long, drooping ears; and wrinkled foreheads.

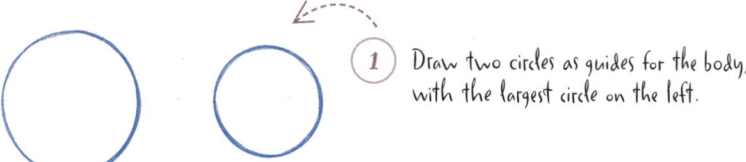

1 Draw two circles as guides for the body, with the largest circle on the left.

2 Add a smaller, oval head shape. Add a horizontal line across the top third and a shorter vertical line.

3 Add an oval for the muzzle and an upside-down Y-shape within it. Add two long, curved lines for the ears – the right ear should overlap the body.

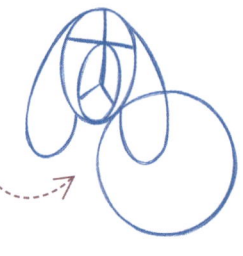

4 Draw four short guidelines for the legs and a small, curved tail.

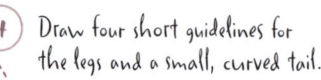

5 Connect the circles using curved lines to form the body.

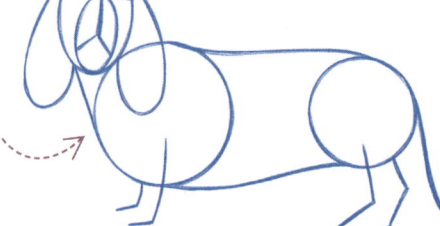

6 Draw the droopy eyes, using the guidelines for placement. Make the top part flatter and the bottom part curvier. Draw the nose within the muzzle guidelines.

7 Draw the mouth using a wavy line under the nose. Add the tongue along the U-shape, and a parallel line for the chin. Draw the ears, making the guidelines curvier and adding folds. Draw the legs and feet, adding some bumps to represent joints. Add a few short lines for toes and nails.

8 Use the connecting lines as guides to draw the rest of the body. Erase your guidelines.

9 Add a mid brown tone over the body, head and ears. Use pale beige for the legs, belly, muzzle and tip of the tail. Add darker brown shading to the back and nose.

10 Add some shading. Colour the eyes brown and the tongue pink.

91

West Highland White Terrier

With their dark, piercing eyes, pointy ears, distinctive white coats
and short, wagging tails, the Westie's looks are simply irresistible.

1. Draw a circle guide, adding a horizontal line across the centre and a shorter, vertical line through the top half. Add a horizontal oval for the muzzle.

2. Add two small, triangular guidelines for the ears.

3. Draw a circle for the body, with two lines under it for the front legs.

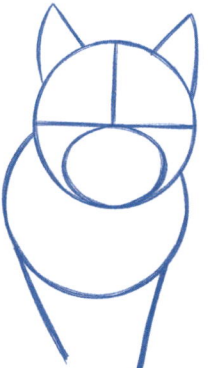

4. Add a small curve linking the body and head shape on the left side for the back, and a little triangle next to the left ear as a tail guide.

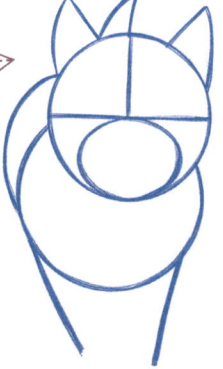

5. Draw two small circles for the eyes. Start drawing the nose in the centre of the muzzle guideline.

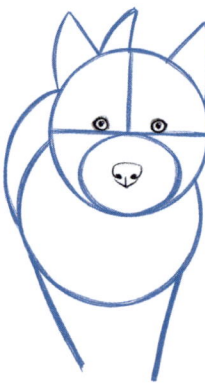

6 Below the nose, draw short strokes for the fur covering the mouth. Draw slightly bigger strokes towards the external sides, following the muzzle guidelines. Trace the lower jaw with two U-shaped lines for the tongue and lips. Add curved strokes for the fur above the eyes.

7 Draw the rest of the head and ears, using short strokes to create fur.

8 Use short strokes around the guidelines for the body, legs and chest.

9 Add little strokes along the curved shape for the back of the body and tail. Erase your guidelines.

10 Use light grey and light brown to give dimension to the white coat. Separate each stroke so the white of the paper comes through and emphasizes the fur-like texture.

Jack Russell Terrier

Jack Russells are lively, independent and clever little dogs, always up to mischief! This one wants to go out and play ball.

1. Draw three circles as guides for the head and body. The top and the bottom circles should be about the same size.

2. Draw a diagonal line across the head at the top as a guide for the eye. Continue the line to create a muzzle shape on the top-right side. Add a round shape for the ear.

3. Draw two lines to the right of the main circle and two below the bottom circle as leg guides.

4. Connect the circles with curved lines to form the body. Add a small circle at the top-right corner for the tennis ball.

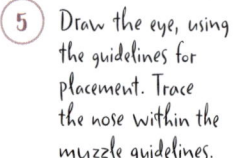

5. Draw the eye, using the guidelines for placement. Trace the nose within the muzzle guidelines.

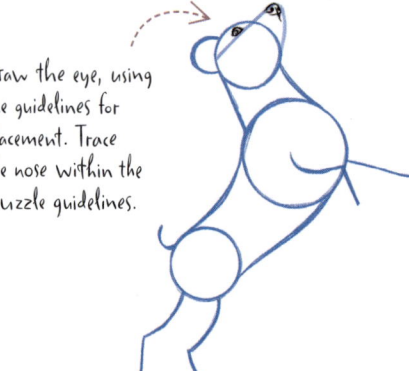

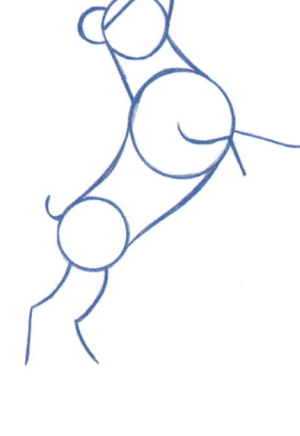

6 Fill in the rest of the muzzle and ear, making the shapes much curvier.

7 Draw a few curved lines along the head circle to represent the forehead. Use guidelines to draw the front and hind legs and feet, adding some bumps to represent joints. Draw a few lines at the bottom for the toes and nails.

8 Use the connecting lines as guides to draw the rest of the body. Add detail to the ball.

9 Erase your guidelines. Start colouring in with a cream base colour and a brown patch on the head.

10 Add some darker tones to your drawing with greys and browns. Add yellow to the tennis ball.

Scottish Terrier

Scotties are solidly compact dogs with vivid personalities and dignified, almost human-like characters. This one looks very proud in his smart collar.

(1) Draw a rectangle as a guide for the body.

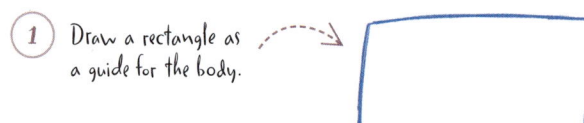

(2) Draw another rectangle on the top-right corner as a guide for the head, and four short, slanted rectangles for the legs.

(3) Draw two tiny triangles for the pointed ears. Continue the vertical line from the right side of the body rectangle through the head shape. Add a straight line for the tail.

(4) Add a small, rectangular collar guide.

(5) Draw the nose tip on the top-right corner of the head rectangle, and the eye at the top of the crossing line.

6   Draw the top part of the muzzle with a curved line going towards the eye. Add longer strokes above the eye to create fluffy eyebrows. Make very long strokes on the lower part of the head.

7   Sketch the leg shapes as you follow the basic path of the guides, using longer strokes at the back of the legs.

8   Draw the rest of the body. Add the collar pendant and tassels. Erase your guidelines.

9   Use jet black around the ears, legs and tail. Add highlights with a lighter tone.

10   Colour the collar in a contrasting shade.

Wirehaired Pointing Griffon

The Griffon's bristly coat is a striking, steel beige colour with chestnut brown markings. This gundog is bright and affectionate with a lively, quick-witted nature.

1 Draw three circle guides for the head and body.

2 Trace a horizontal line towards the top of the head circle. Add a narrow triangle on the right side for the ear and another on the left for the top of the muzzle.

3 Draw two long, vertical guidelines under each circle for the legs (a). Trace a longer diagonal for one of the hind legs (b), which is stretched. Draw a line for the tail (c).

(a)   (b)   (c)

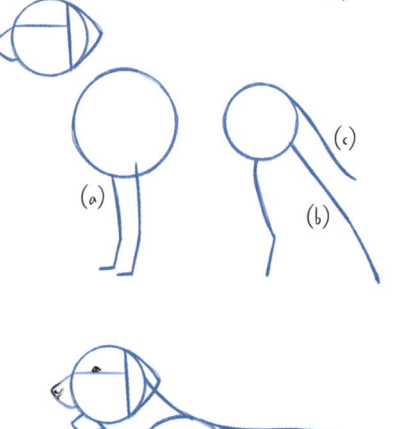

4 Draw lines to connect the body circles. Add the lower part of the muzzle to the bottom left of the head. Draw a shape underneath for the rock.

5 Sketch a small circle for the eye, using the horizontal line as a guide. Draw the nose at the tip of the muzzle.

6 Continue drawing the muzzle, with short, curved strokes above and below the nose. Add a couple of lines for the eyebrow. Trace the ear with short strokes.

7 Follow the guides to draw the head and legs, adding the toes and nails under the front legs.

8 Darken the guidelines to create the overall body shape, making the lines more curved. Add a collar.

9 Trace the rock with wobbly lines and add a few strokes on top for the grass. Erase your guidelines. Add colour, with a light beige body and muzzle, mid brown head, chin and ears, and little spots of brown on the back. Use light pink for the tongue and nose.

10 Add darker brown tones on the face, grey tones on the rock and green for the grass.

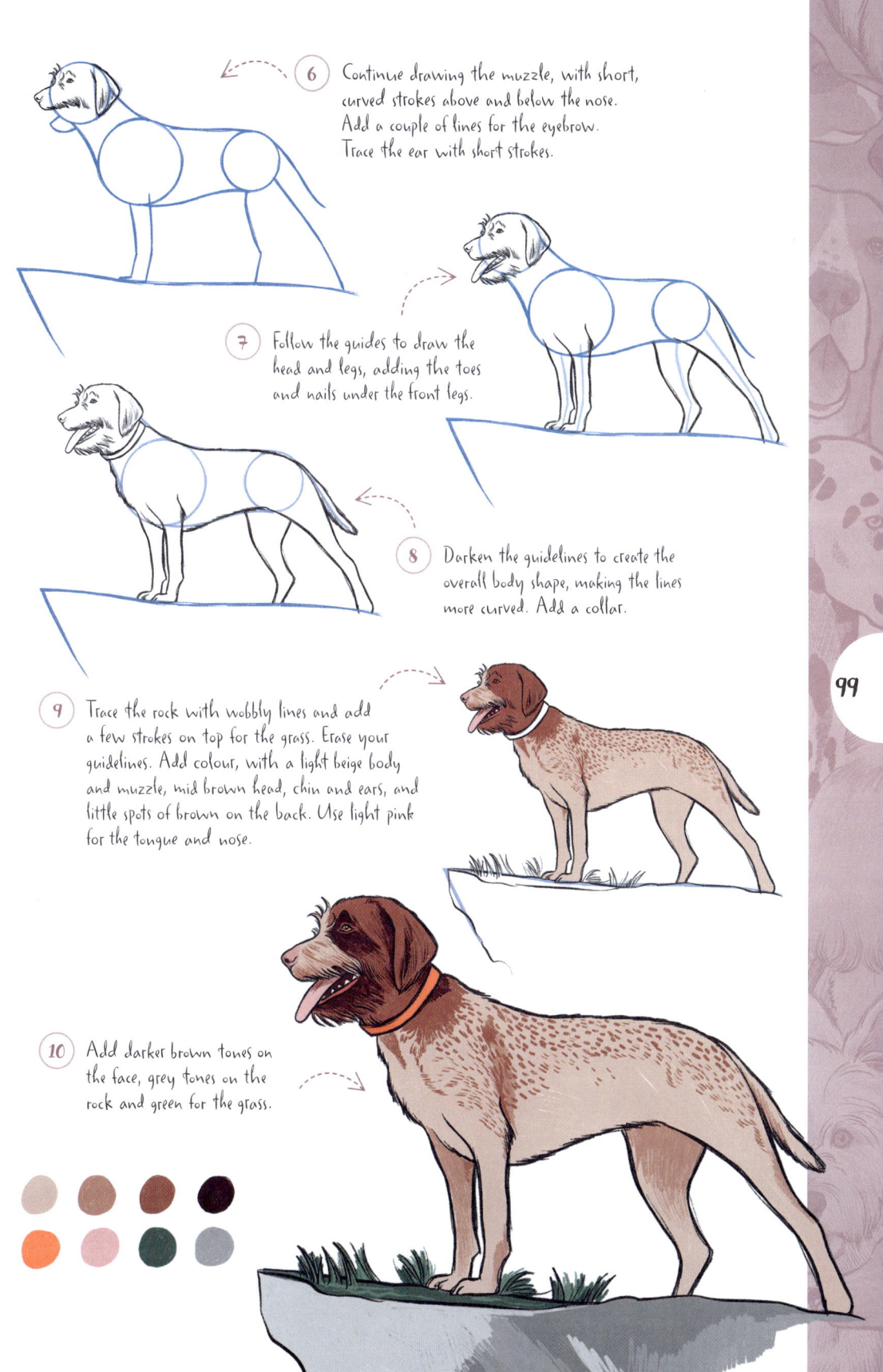

Dalmatian

Use long, smooth lines as you follow the basic path of your guidelines here,
as the Dalmatian's distinctive, spotty coat is short, satiny and fine.

1 Draw three circle guides for the body and head.

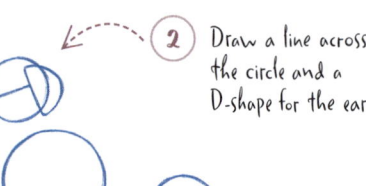

2 Draw a line across the circle and a D-shape for the ear.

3 Draw a muzzle shape at the tip of the horizontal line, curving back to the bottom of the head circle. Add a circle for the ball. Add guidelines for the legs, bending them two-thirds of the way down for the joints.

4 Trace neck and body lines to join all the shapes together. Add a tail, slightly curving it at the tip.

5 Draw the eye along the horizontal line and sketch the nose at the tip of the muzzle.

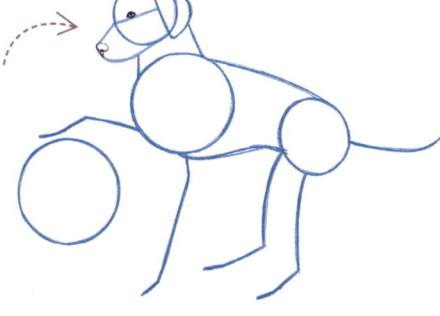

6 Use the muzzle shape to draw the nose and mouth, and the D-shape to draw the ear.

7 Use the guidelines to draw the legs, adding toes and nails. Trace the ball.

8 Finish tracing the body. Erase your guidelines.

9 Add an off-white or light beige base colour, and some very light green or blue for the eye.

10 Add some well-defined dense black or deep brown spots all over the coat. These will be slightly bigger on the back and smaller on the face and legs. Add shading under the belly and neck. Colour the ball bright red and add a cast shadow.

Irish Wolfhound

One of the tallest dog breeds, Irish Wolfhounds have a wild mane,
so do not be afraid to use long, messy strokes in your drawing.

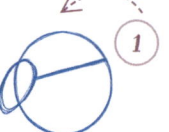

1 Draw a circle guide, with a horizontal line across. Add a small, overlapping oval for the ear.

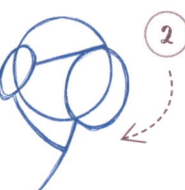

2 Draw an oval on the lower right as a muzzle guide. Trace a large U-shape for the front of the body. Add a collar line.

3 Add another, larger U-shape to the top left, with a vertical line through the centre.

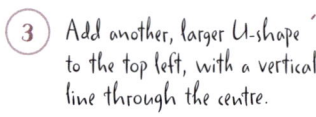

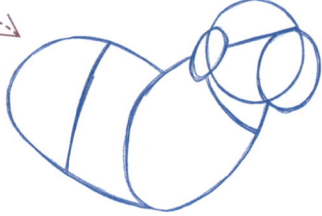

4 Trace three guidelines for the legs, adding small circles for feet. Draw a tail line.

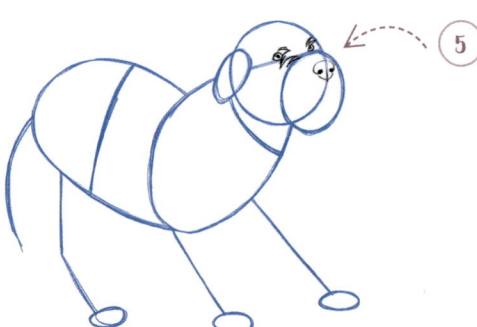

5 Draw the eyes by lightly sketching some hairlines, then adding small circles under them. Draw the nose inside the muzzle, along the circle guideline. Draw a small, vertical line at the bottom and shade the nostrils.

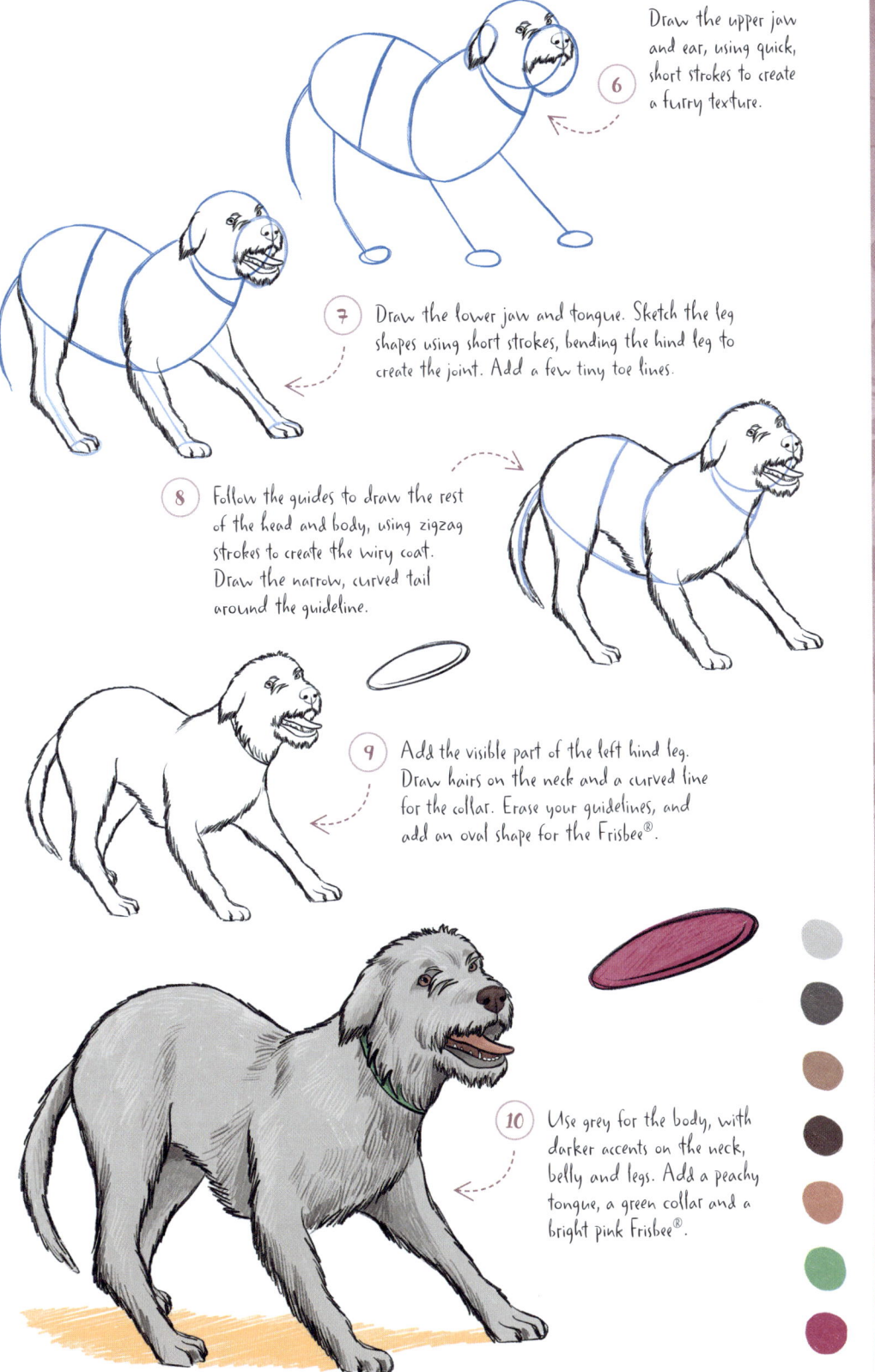

Draw the upper jaw and ear, using quick, short strokes to create a furry texture.

6

7 Draw the lower jaw and tongue. Sketch the leg shapes using short strokes, bending the hind leg to create the joint. Add a few tiny toe lines.

8 Follow the guides to draw the rest of the head and body, using zigzag strokes to create the wiry coat. Draw the narrow, curved tail around the guideline.

9 Add the visible part of the left hind leg. Draw hairs on the neck and a curved line for the collar. Erase your guidelines, and add an oval shape for the Frisbee®.

10 Use grey for the body, with darker accents on the neck, belly and legs. Add a peachy tongue, a green collar and a bright pink Frisbee®.

Bull Terrier

These, mischievous, highly energetic, muscular dogs can be distinguished by their long, egg-shaped heads. They thrive on affection and exercise.

1. Draw a circle guide. Add a straight, horizontal line towards the top, extending it out on the left side. Add two triangular ears.

2. Draw a line on each side of the horizontal line to create the profile. Add an oval shape for the body.

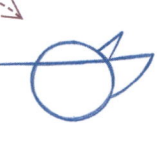

3. Draw two short, vertical lines for the front legs and two guidelines for the hind legs. Bend the lines to indicate the joints and feet.

4. Draw two small, connecting lines for the neck and a curved tail.

5. Sketch the eye on the horizontal line and the nose at the tip of the muzzle.

6 Draw two curved lines for the lips. Use the triangle guides to draw the ears, making them more wavy on the sides. Add short strokes within the shapes for the inner ear structure.

7 Follow the guidelines to sketch the shape of the legs. The front-left leg is slightly raised. Bend the hind leg near the top for the joint. Add short lines for toes and triangles for nails.

8 Draw the rest of the body. Erase your guidelines.

9 Add an off white base colour for the front part and paws, and mid brown for the face, ears and back.

10 Add some shading to give your drawing more dimension and volume, using strokes that go in the general direction of the fur.

Akita

The fearless, large, powerful Akita has a noble, intimidating presence, originally bred for guarding royalty in feudal Japan.

1. Draw a circle guide, with a smaller circle within it.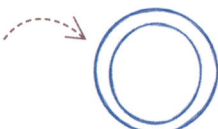

2. Sketch two triangular ears, starting on the smaller circle and ending on the larger one. Add two crossing lines within the smaller circle.

3. Add a tiny circle for the nose. Draw a large rectangle for the body.

4. Draw a curly tail. Add four lines for legs, with small circles for the paws.

5. Sketch two tiny ovals for the eyes, using the guidelines for placement. Draw the nose inside the small circle. Add two curved lines for the top lips.

6 Give the ears structure. Draw quick, short strokes inside each ear for the fur within. Draw the bottom part of the muzzle, with the tongue popping out.

7 Sketch the leg shapes as you follow the guidelines. Add curved lines for the toes.

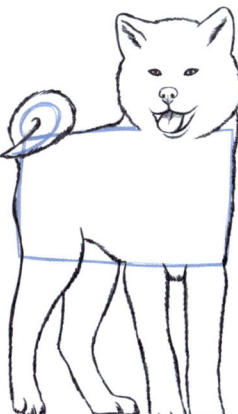

8 Draw the rest of the body and tail, using quick, short strokes for a fuzzy texture. Erase your guidelines. Add small strokes around your drawing to create fur.

9 Start with an off-white base colour. Use orange for the main markings of the coat, brown for the eyes and nose, and pink for the tongue.

10 Add darker values through the coat to give it dimension. Finally, add some pink ground shadow.

Afghan Hound

The Afghan is elegance personified with its luxurious silky coat, exotic face and model-like stature. It is a breed that is sure to turn heads.

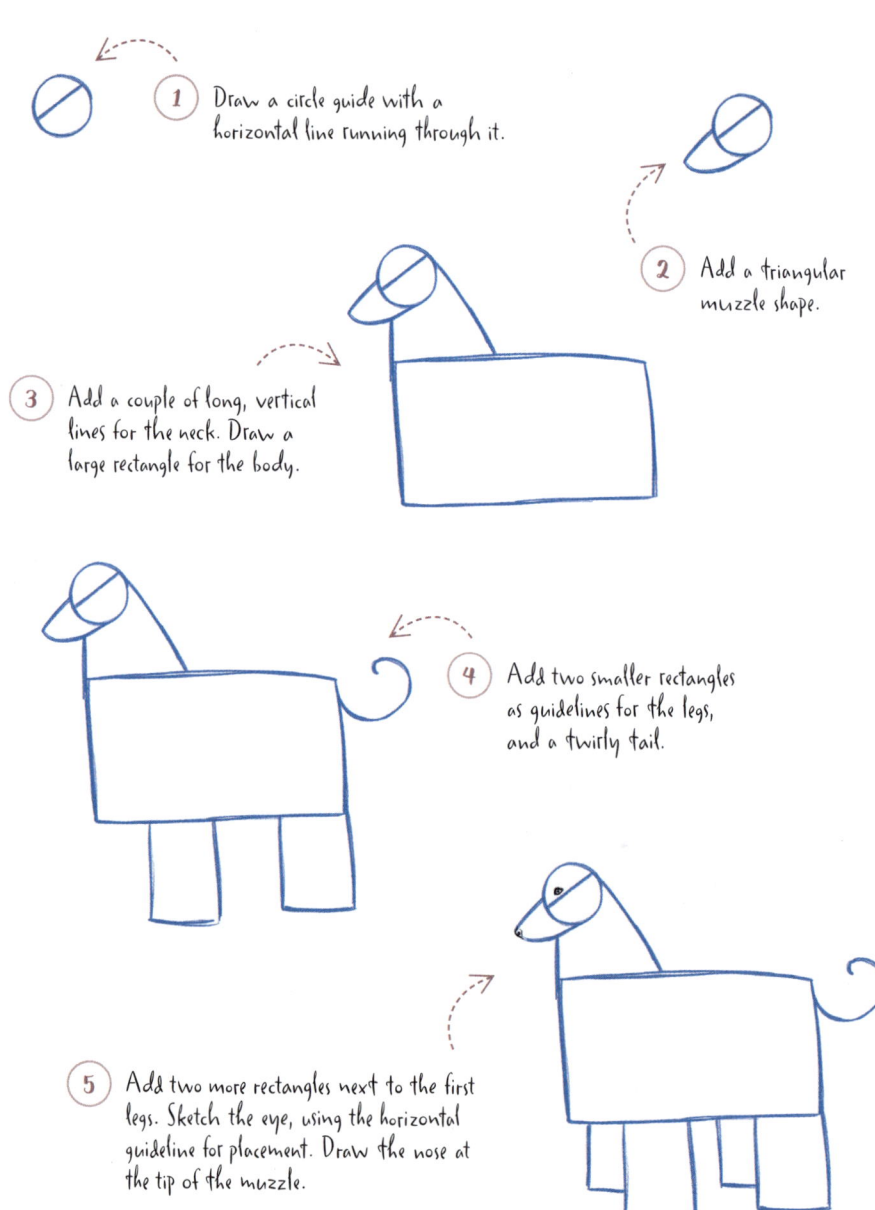

1 Draw a circle guide with a horizontal line running through it.

2 Add a triangular muzzle shape.

3 Add a couple of long, vertical lines for the neck. Draw a large rectangle for the body.

4 Add two smaller rectangles as guidelines for the legs, and a twirly tail.

5 Add two more rectangles next to the first legs. Sketch the eye, using the horizontal guideline for placement. Draw the nose at the tip of the muzzle.

6 Continue drawing the muzzle with short, curved strokes above and below the nose. Add a few curved lines around the eye.

7 Follow the basic guidelines to darken the head. Use extra-long strokes to create the ear. Follow the guides to fill in the legs.

8 Draw the rest of the body, using very long, wavy strokes to create the long hair.

9 Erase your guidelines. Add a light, sandy base colour.

10 Add some shading with light and dark brown tones.

Dogs & puppies

Beagle

Small, fun-loving and hardy, Beagle pups are active companions. They are never happier than when following an interesting scent or chasing a ball.

1. Draw a circle guide, adding a horizontal line across the centre and a curved, vertical line through the top-left half.

2. Draw a smaller circle overlapping the lower, left side as a muzzle guide. Add a D-shaped ear.

3. Trace a loaf-like body shape. Add four guidelines for the legs and a curved tail.

4. Draw two small, almond-shaped eyes, using the guides for placement. The right eye should be a little bigger than the left. Add the nose.

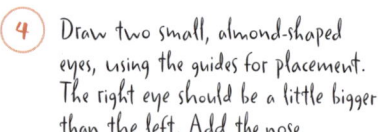

5. Draw a line from the top of the nose to the eye on the left, and one that starts under the nose then curves to the right, staying inside the small circle. Add a ball in the mouth and a couple of curved lines for the chin.

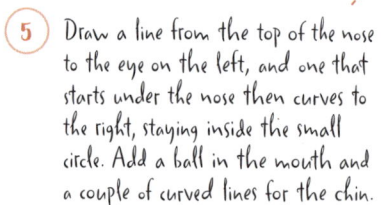

6 Follow the main circle to draw the rest of the head. Add a couple of lines for the neck.

7 Follow the guidelines to sketch the front legs. Add short, curved lines for toes.

8 Draw the hind legs. Curve the legs as the guide bends to represent the joints. The top part should be thicker than the bottom. Add short, curved lines for the toes.

9 Erase your guidelines. Add a very light grey base colour, light brown on the head and dark grey on the back and tail. The eyes are light brown and the nose is dark grey.

10 Add shadow to the forehead, neck, chest and belly. Colour the ball red and the tongue, front pad and toe nails pink. Add strokes of green grass around the feet.

Golden Retriever

This gorgeous Golden Retriever is looking lovingly at her young pup. You can use longer strokes if you want to draw them with shaggier fur.

1 Draw a circle guide for the pup's head and a slightly larger circle for the body. To the top left, add an oval shape for the mother's head.

2 Add a guide for the pup's muzzle (a), two straight leg shapes and circles for paws. Add a horizontal line across the mother's head, and cross it with a vertical line on the lower half (b). Add two triangular ears and a larger circle for the chest.

3 Add curved lines for the pup's neck and hind legs. Add circles for the hind paws and a horizontal, U-shaped tail. Trace lines for the rest of the mother's body and tail.

4 Add a U-shape for the pup's ear. Trace a long, straight line under the chest circle for the mother's left front leg.

5 Draw the pup's eye adjacent to the top of the muzzle and the mother's eyes on each side of the vertical line. Use the guides to draw the ears with quick, short strokes. Add the mother's nose at the tip of the vertical line.

6 Add detail to the pup's muzzle.

7 Sketch the leg shapes as you follow the guides. Add a few curved lines for toes.

8 Use the remaining guidelines to draw the rest of the dogs' bodies and tails using quick, short strokes. Erase your guidelines.

9 Add a light beige base colour, using a lighter tone for the pup. Colour the eyes and nose dark brown.

10 Add darker tones around the ears, necks and bellies.

Great Dane

Known as 'gentle giants', Great Danes look very imposing but have the sweetest nature. This mother stands proudly with her pup at her side.

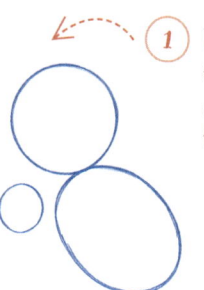

1 Draw two circle guides for the mother's body and a smaller circle for the pup's head.

2 Add a smaller circle for the mother's head, with curved, intersecting lines and a small circle for the muzzle. Add two intersecting lines on the pup's head, and a small circle for the muzzle.

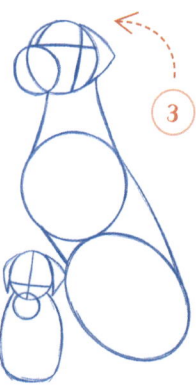

3 Add triangles for the ears. Draw curved lines connecting the three circles to complete the mother's neck and body, and add a U-shape for the pup's body.

4 Draw a long, curved tail on the bottom right. Add guidelines for the legs, bending the hind legs to indicate the joints for the feet.

5 Sketch small circles for the eyes with tiny, central C-shapes for the pupils. The mother's right eye should be smaller because of the way the head is turned. Draw the noses, adding two oval nostrils and a small, vertical line to split them at the bottom.

6 Draw the ears with short strokes. Draw the top lips as long, wavy lines that start under the nose and extend to the bottom edge of the circle guide.

7 Sketch the front legs around the guides, bulging the shapes out around the joints. Add short, curved lines for the toes, with tiny triangles for nails.

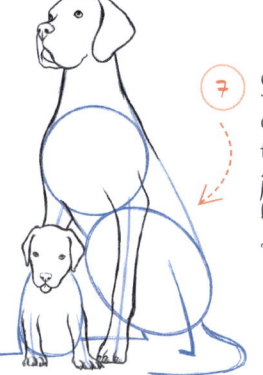

8 Add the hind legs, toes and claws.

9 Finish tracing the dogs' bodies and the mother's tail. Erase your guidelines.

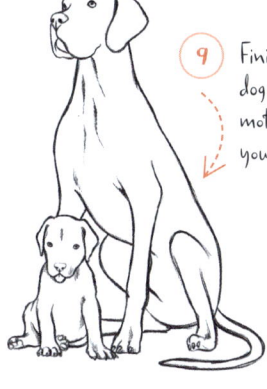

10 Colour the mother with an off white coat, adding dark grey spots, and the pup in grey. Add some shading to give your dogs more dimension.

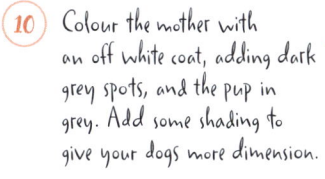

Corgi

Corgis are bright, sensitive, loyal dogs, equipped for a hard day's work with their short, powerful legs. However, this pup looks ready for a nap!

1 Draw a circle guide for the head and a smaller overlapping circle for the muzzle.

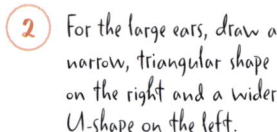

2 For the large ears, draw a narrow, triangular shape on the right and a wider U-shape on the left.

3 Draw a circle, two or three times bigger than the head, for the body.

4 Draw two ovals for the thighs and two smaller ovals for the paws on the left side of the body. Add two more ovals as front leg guides.

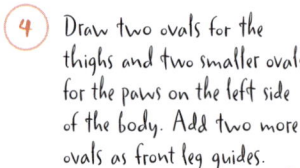

5 Sketch two small, pointed, football-shaped eyes. Draw a small oval for the nose inside the muzzle.

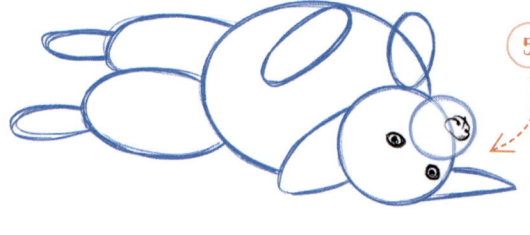

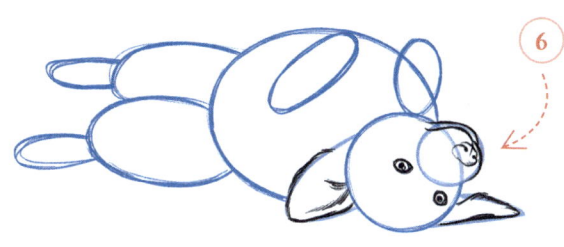

6 Follow the edge of the small circle guide to create the outer shape of the muzzle. Draw the ears in a wavy shape with rounded tips. Add a few quick, short strokes within the left ear for the furry opening.

7 Draw the front and hind legs, using quick, short strokes.

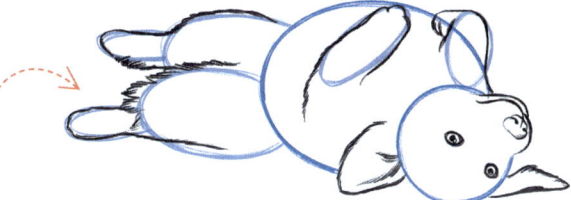

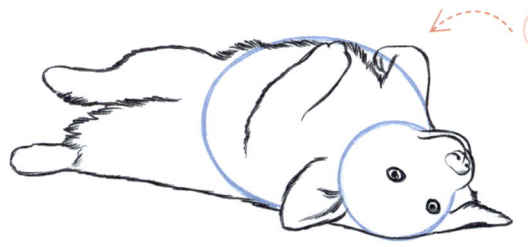

8 Use quick, short strokes to darken the outer edges of the initial guides to create the body shape. Use slightly longer strokes for the longer fur on the underside. Erase your guidelines.

9 The muzzle, eye area, chest, underside and legs should be kept white. Colour the rest of the body with an orange tone.

10 Add some shading to the coat, using values that vary from medium to dark to emphasize shadows and highlights.

Collie

These sensitive, affectionate dogs have beautiful, multicoloured coats of long, rough-textured fur. Draw with long strokes to depict the long hair.

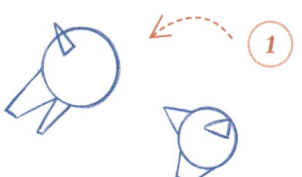

1 Draw two circle guides for the heads, making the right one smaller. Add triangular shapes for the ears and angular shapes for the muzzles.

2 Draw two circle guides for the pup's body, with the right one smaller than the left, about the same size as the head. Add a large circle for the mother's body.

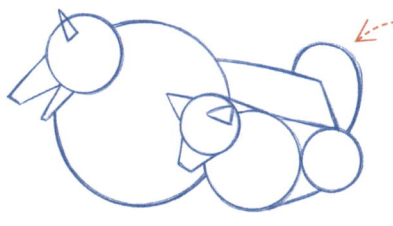

3 Add lines to connect the circles to form the pup's body. Draw a rectangular shape on the right side of the mother's body circle and a curved tail shape.

4 Draw lines for the pup's legs, bending the hind legs to indicate the joints. For the mother, draw two straight lines at the front and add a third beneath the pup's belly.

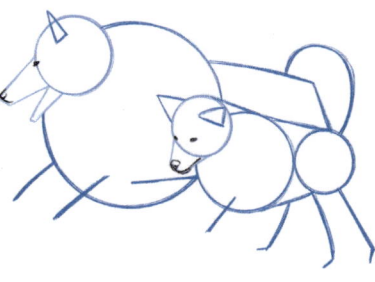

5 Draw both dogs' eyes and noses along the guidelines.

6 Draw the triangular ears. Link them to the tips of the noses and finish with the bottom jaws.

7 Sketch the legs around the guidelines, bending them to indicate joints. Draw the paws, using short, curved lines for the toes.

8 Follow the guidelines to draw the rest of each dog. Some of the adult dog is hidden behind the puppy.

9 Erase your guidelines. Add an off white base colour with some shading on the pup. Colour the noses in dark grey and the mother's tongue in pink.

10 Add an orange tone to the heads, bodies and legs. Finally, add some ground shadow.

Bull Terrier

Bull Terrier puppies have the sleekest, shiniest coats.
These adorable pups look like friends for life.

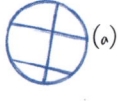

1 Draw two circle guides for the heads with vertical lines through the centre. For the first circle, add two horizontal lines (a). For the second circle, add one horizontal line and a circular muzzle guide (b).

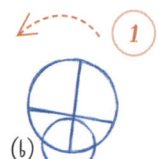

2 For the first circle, add a triangular ear and a semicircle for the nose guide. Add a U-shape as a guide for the yawning lower jaw. For the second circle, add two triangular ears and make the lower part of the muzzle squarish, with two bent lines on either side.

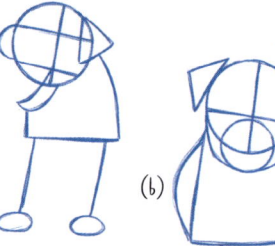

3 Draw the body shapes and straight lines for the front legs. As the second dog is lying down, the legs will be shorter (a). Add a small curve on the left of this body shape for the belly (b).

4 Draw another curve for the second pup's back (a). Add a line with a circle at its tip and another small circle to its right for the hind legs (b). Add a straight line on the right side of the first pup, linking it to the second pup (c), and two more lines to complete its body (d).

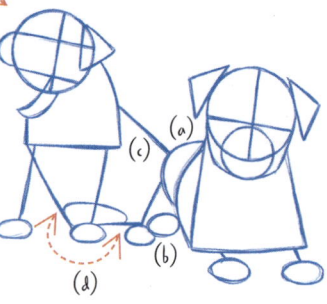

5 Draw both dogs' eyes and noses along the guidelines.

6 Add detail around the noses and the ears, and the first pup's lower jaw and tongue. Trace the second pup's head outline with short, smooth strokes.

7 Sketch the leg shapes around the guides, using short strokes and adding curves for the toes.

8 Draw the remainder of the dogs, adding short curves to create the skin folds. Erase your guidelines.

9 Colour the first pup in a sandy tone and the second in warm brown. Add a light patch on each chest.

10 Use darker tones to create dimension. Use a light blue for the eyes and brown tones for the noses. Add some green grass below.

Irish Setter

This energetic, inquisitive mother and pup look like they are enjoying a run in the grass. Their rich mahogany coats look beautiful in the sunlight.

1 Draw two circle guides for the heads, with the smallest for the pup on the left. Add a horizontal line crossing each circle.

2 For the pup, add a triangle-like shape to the left for the ear (a) and a D-shape on the right for the muzzle (b). For the mother, add a squarish shape for the ear (c) and two shapes for the open muzzle (d).

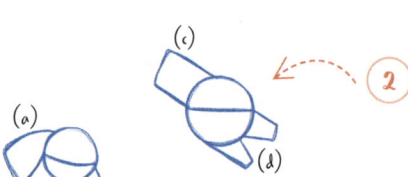

3 Draw a rectangular shape under the pup's head, and two straight lines coming from the mother's head.

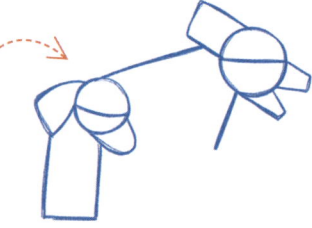

4 Add another straight line to continue the mother's body. Draw two lines for the front legs. For the puppy, draw a bent right front leg.

5 Draw a series of curved lines to create the back of the dogs. Add four lines at the back of the puppy for the two hind legs, the tail and one of the mother's hind legs. Draw both dogs' eyes and noses along the guidelines.

6 Draw the ears. Add detail to the tip of the nose and bottom jaw.

7 Sketch the leg shapes around the guides, bending the lines to indicate joints. Add the paws using short, curved lines for the toes. Create some grass with short strokes.

8 Use the guidelines to draw the rest of the dogs.

9 Erase your guidelines. Add a bright orange base colour.

10 Finalize your drawing with darker shading of red and chestnut tones. Colour the grass green.

Cocker Spaniel

This naughty puppy has been caught chewing on his owner's slipper!
With those adorable eyes and cute floppy ears, he is sure to be forgiven.

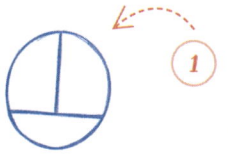

1 Draw a circle guide, adding a horizontal line across the bottom third and a vertical line through the centre.

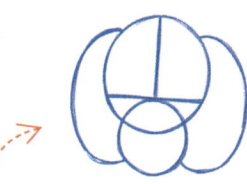

2 Draw a smaller circle, overlapping the bottom half of the head as a muzzle guide. Draw two long arcs for the ears.

3 Add a triangular chest, with two straight lines under it for the front legs. Trace a loaf-like body shape.

4 Add the right hind leg, bent halfway, and a tail line. Draw a bean shape for the slipper.

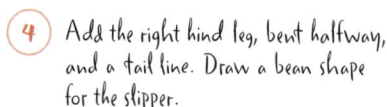

5 Draw the almost-triangular eyes, using the guidelines for placement. Add tiny reflection circles at each side and bigger dots in the middle for pupils. Trace the nose at the bottom of the muzzle guideline, shading in two smaller circles for nostrils.

6 Draw the rest of the muzzle using smooth lines. Use quick, short strokes for the furry ears, adding a few strokes inside for more texture.

7 Use the guidelines to draw the front and hind legs with quick, short strokes.

8 Draw the body with smoother lines. Sketch the slipper.

9 Erase your guidelines. Add small strokes to create a soft fur effect on the coat.

10 Colour the body with a light tan tone. Add light orange accents to the eyebrows, ears and sides of the legs. Use darker brown shading around the neck, between the eyes and on the inside of the legs. The eyes will be light green.

About the artist

Justine Lecouffe is an illustrator, designer and storyboard artist based in London, UK. Her work focuses on digital illustration, graphic design and some dabbling in motion media. Themes of femininity, beauty and nature often dominate her work, making it the perfect fit for clients in the fashion, jewellery and cosmetic sectors. She specializes in design and illustration, but has a long and ambitious wish list of styles and genres to master. When she's not drawing, you can find her cooking comfort food, cycling around London, snapping film photos or simply scrolling dog and cat memes.

If you'd like to find out more information or see further examples of her work, find Justine on Instagram @justine_lcf.

Acknowledgements

Many thanks to all the readers of *10-Step Drawing: People* and *10-Step Drawing: Everyday Things,* who gave me such positive feedback. This was wonderful encouragement and pushed me to draw for this third publication. And I'm again immensely grateful to the team at The Bright Press for another fantastic opportunity and their brilliant support throughout the project.